RISING ABOVE ANGER

A believer's guide to overcoming hurts, hatred, and desires for revenge

Presented by E. Lonnie Melashenko
Written by David B. Smith

Pacific Press® Publishing Association
Nampa, Idaho
Oshawa, Ontario, Canada
www.pacificpress.com

Edited by Jerry D. Thomas
Designed by Dennis Feree
Cover photo by Bryan Reinhart / Masterfile

Copyright © 2001 by

Pacific Press® Publishing Association
Printed in the United States of America
All Rights Reserved

Additional copies of this book may be purchased at
http://www.adventistbookcenter.com

ISBN 0-8163-1855-7

01 02 03 04 05 • 5 4 3 2 1

Contents

How Long Should You Hold a Hand Grenade?

"I'm so mad I could just pop that guy!" It's amazing how quickly, how suddenly, our tempers can flare. In the flash of a moment, some injustice done, some wrong act committed against us, makes us mad. And guess what? The Bible says that kind of anger isn't wrong.

The book is a *tour de force*. The film is an Oscar-winning *tour de force*. *Dead Man Walking,* by Sister Helen Prejean, was portrayed on the screen by actors Sean Penn and Susan Sarandon. It's a powerful study of the death penalty in America, and this devout Catholic nun finds herself rather decidedly on one side of the war.

There are so many stories of heinous crimes in this book: mass murders, murders involving rape, murders involving torture. Young girls are suddenly gone from the little country houses they lived in all their lives; Mom and Dad wait and wait, while the police scour the countryside. A young man's graduation robe hangs in the closet, unworn, unused. Senior prom photos on the kitchen table. And finally the horrible news comes in: "Mr. and Mrs. LeBlanc, I'm sorry . . . we found David's body."

What makes the anger of these parents even greater is that when they get to the courtroom, or when they go to Angola, the penitentiary, they see Sister Helen there with the man who killed their child! She's there with Patrick Sonnier, praying with him, comforting him, fighting for a stay of execution. It almost seems like the church, and by extension, God, is on the enemy side, aiding and abetting, helping to prolong their torture.

Sister Prejean describes the experience of a couple whose daughter was abducted, raped, and murdered. It took several days to find the decomposed body out in the woods, and police needed a positive ID. They thought it would be too much for the parents, so the mother's brother, who was a dentist, went to the funeral home and confirmed from dental restorations that it was his niece.

And the dad said later: "Elizabeth's brother was pretty tore up when he came back from the funeral home. Before he reached his hand into that bag with all the lime in it and fished out Faith's jaw, he said he had always been against the death penalty. But, boy, after that, he was for it."

This volume you hold is a blending of three radio series. The most recent is: "I've Got to Nurse This Grudge Because It's SICK!" There's also a five-part sermon series entitled "I Can't Stop HATING You!" a word twist on the old country-western hit by Hank Williams. And finally, "What to Do About Loving Hatred."

Most of us can quickly say, "Been there, done that" to all three of these human scenarios. We've felt that gnawing, repeated, never-ending, haunting-your-dreams hatred of that certain some-one. That person who hurt you. That person who has always profited at your expense. That person who has cheated his or her way to the head of the line, and always by taking the spot you should have had.

The *Los Angeles Times,* in its sports section, once described the emotional state of a woman whose husband had formerly owned a professional NFL football team. After his death some time ago, it came out publicly that he had had a series of extra-marital affairs. His wife had never known —and now this sordid little pile of adventures had come to light.

What were her thoughts about what her husband had done? He was already dead and buried and lying in the ground. Was that enough? Was the fact that he was gone sufficient to cool down her anger and resentment? No. "I'd like to pull him out of the grave," she said, "and shoot him with every bullet I could get."

I think just about every single person on this planet would like to change just that one word in Hank Williams's country hit, and sing it: "I can't stop HATING you." That expression—those five words—are helplessly real. "I can't stop!" People have tried; they truly have tried to forgive or to repress or to submerge their feelings for this particular person. Maybe they've gone to a small group fellowship or gotten counseling or undergone encounter therapy, tried to get in touch with their anger. (Although most of us are plenty enough "in touch" with our anger.) Maybe they've even packed up and moved across the country in order to try the old "Out of sight, out of mind" kind of treatment.

And yet that revised song stays right on top of the pop music charts of our psyche: "I can't stop HATING you; it's useless to try."

What can we do with hate? Does the Christian faith teach us anything about hate? Does it provide answers that are any better, any more successful, than what gets vended on talk radio and self-help books?

The Bible certainly does talk about hatred and it shares principles that are supposed to work. But even the best of Christians experience very little success at applying the strategies outlined in the Word of God. Believers often walk around just as mad and red in the face as the general population. But that's not the fault of the principles. It really boils down to two things: our unwillingness and the enormity of the problem. Unresolved rage is simply a blockbuster temptation, an incredibly successful tool of our enemy.

I don't know if it's comforting or not to discover that people in the Bible—even some of the Bible writers—were in this very same boat. Have you read some of the psalms? When you get away from Psalm 23 and all the still waters and grassy-green meadows, some of the rest of King David's writing happens in rip-roaring rapids and poison pastures instead. Philip Yancey, in his latest book about the Old Testament, entitled *The Bible Jesus Read,* writes: "You don't have to read far in Psalms before encountering some troubling passages, furious outbursts hidden like landmines in the midst of soothing pastoral poetry. Some seem on the level of 'I hope you get hit by a truck!' schoolyard epithets. 'Imprecatory psalms,' these are called, or sometimes 'vindictive psalms,' or, more bluntly, 'cursing psalms' because of the curses they rain down on opponents."

The dictionary tells us that an imprecation is a calling down of a curse on someone else's head. It's essentially a screaming rant-and-rave. "You stupid, ugly so-and-so, I hope your dog dies! I hope your house blows away in a hurricane! I hope your cable TV goes out during the Super Bowl!"

Do you think I'm kidding? Here's Psalm 3:7: *"Arise, O Lord! Deliver me, O my God! Strike all my enemies on the jaw; break the teeth of the wicked."*

Most of this kind of writing actually goes along the vein of

"Lord, please, just shut them up. Somehow express, in a voice from heaven, that I've been right and they've been wrong. All I want is justice."

The Bible tells many stories that show us simmering rage and resentment. A classic is the Genesis saga of Jacob and Esau, twin brothers who hated each other. And with good reason, when Jacob ripped off his older brother's "birthright," or spiritual inheritance. Then he went on to trick his blind and aging father, Isaac, even putting animal fur on his arms so he'd feel as hairy as Esau. And when Older Brother discovered he'd been swindled, he vowed bloody mayhem and vengeance; Jacob had to head out at midnight to Haran or Paddan Aram in northwest Mesopotamia. His brother, it says in Genesis 27:41, " . . . held a grudge against Jacob because of the blessing his father had given him. He said to himself, 'The days of mourning for my father are near; then I will kill my brother Jacob.' "

Skip down about five chapters to Genesis 32, to a scenario that's a full twenty years later! And what do we find? The grudge is still on! Mama had promised her son, "Don't worry, honey. When Esau stops hating you, I'll send for you and you can come home" . . . and twenty years later, she'd never sent that telegram. Esau's resentment against his little brother is simmering just as strong as two decades earlier; in fact, he's coming down the freeway toward him with a personal army of 400 men!

Fortunately, as you read the story, Jacob demonstrates true repentance and humility, plus he has a huge present for Esau, God intervenes, and there's no bloodshed. But even in Bible times, there was certainly such a thing as blood feuds and long-standing resentment. "I can't stop hating you" was Esau's theme song for sure.

Centuries later, as we read through the book of 1 Samuel, a

9

new monarch named Saul, the first king of Israel, struggles with hate; in fact, it's his worst liability. He hates David, the Goliath-killer; he hates the songs all the pretty girls sing about this top warrior in Israel: "Saul has slain his thousands, and David his tens of thousands."

What king wouldn't resent a hit record like that playing all across Israel on every radio station? And soon "I can't stop hating you" became his mantra as well. Various versions of the Bible use words like "angry," "jealous," "depressed." Face it, Saul nursed a resentment that just wouldn't go away, even though young David was a huge blessing to him personally with his military prowess and spiritual maturity. As good as David was in Saul's administration, Saul simply couldn't stop hating. Finally, he picked up a spear and tried to literally pin his enemy to the palace wall with it; in fact, he tried the same desperate, rage-inspired stunt twice. (Not a smart thing to do when David is ten times better at spear-chucking.)

Well, maybe spears aren't flying at your face at work or at home—although perhaps you're tempted to toss a few, at least verbal ones. But what things are triggering our resentment, our nine-lives kinds of hatred that just plain won't go away and die?

In an article entitled "Handling Anger on the Job," author Susan Bixler shares with readers in the magazine *Management Digest* fourteen sure-fire anger triggers. Here they are:

1. Having a boss or co-worker regularly critique your appearance.
2. Being stood up for an appointment.
3. Being unfairly criticized without the opportunity to respond.
4. Being deliberately lied to.

5. Observing discourteous treatment of your secretary or assistant.

6. Watching a co-worker show flagrant disregard of established rules.

7. Getting stuck with the "household chores."

8. Working with someone who refuses to admit mistakes.

9. Dealing with someone who constantly interrupts you in meetings and in the middle of conversations.

10. Having an associate finish your sentences for you.

11. Enduring habitual lateness.

12. Listening to endless chatter about subjects not related to business.

13. Having a confidence betrayed.

14. Having someone make you look inept, uninformed, or downright stupid in front of others.

Any one of those could make you mad, but some people honestly feel like they're dealing with all fourteen on a seven-days-a-week basis. A few years ago, when the Voice of Prophecy did a radio message entitled "God's Christmas Card to Dilbert," many listeners responded: "Boy, can I relate to this!" Frustration and continuous resentment are very, very familiar human conditions.

What do we do when the problem in our life simply isn't going to go away? Maybe it's your boss—and he simply isn't leaving. He's not going to retire, he's not going to move, he's not going to get run over by a cement truck. You hand him that Dilbert cartoon strip, and he doesn't realize you're giving him a message. He just doesn't "get it." And this person is obviously in your life to stay; he's a fixture.

Or maybe it's a co-worker. Or a parent or a spouse or a child. Or your divorced mate, who now lives one block over with his new little girlfriend . . . and they're in church together every weekend. Talk about resentment and the country-western choir song: "I Can't Stop HATING You!"

Well, as the Christian studies this difficult topic and thinks about Saul and Dilbert, Concept One is a simple one: **It is not wrong to get angry.**

That's it. It's not a sin to have anger in your heart. Did you know that? Ephesians 4:26 says it very plainly: " 'In your anger do not sin.' "

It's interesting that Paul is quoting here from . . . guess what source? That's right, the book of Psalms. In fact, that line—"In your anger do not sin"—is just five verses later from David's sock-'em-in-the-jaw diatribe. But the Word of God—Psalms 4 and Ephesians 4—tells us that there is a time and a place when anger is not a wrong emotion.

That's got to be comforting to some of the people in Sister Helen Prejean's case studies, which she shares in *Dead Man Walking*. She was fighting the death penalty for all she was worth. She was trying to rescue those men on Death Row. But she also came to realize the incredible pain, the overwhelming anger, being felt by the victims. She began to see the hurting folks sitting on the other side of the courtroom, the people who were desperately waiting for the state to throw the electric switch to end their misery. Their grudges were a crippling burden.

She tells about a man named Jimmy Christian, who was told by the police, back in 1988, that his son had been killed. Did the cops ever get back to him? Did the authorities stay in touch? Not one word. He eventually heard "on the streets" that somebody had been arrested.

Another victim, Johnny Johnson, came home from church one day and found his wife dead. Her throat cut. The only thing the police did was to arrest him for the crime, even though his innocence was ironclad and obvious.

Mildred Brewer actually saw her own daughter get shot one day, back in 1979. But instead of getting to ride in the ambulance to the hospital with her kid, police hauled her off to headquarters and wasted three hours grilling *her*. During those three hours, her daughter died. When the police finally arrested someone, the DA never even bothered to phone Mrs. Brewer to tell her.

And of course, these stories are multiplied over and over, some in agonizing detail. Parents would wait for long, horrifying years while the killers of their children played the system, filing one appeal after another. Television headlines mocked them night after night. It was a brutal ride, the emotional roller coaster.

It's no wonder that Sister Helen and these grieving, angry, poverty-stricken victims, in their twelve-step meetings with names like "Survive," came up with really the only slogan that made any sense: *God makes a way out of no way.*

So some anger isn't wrong. Someone cheats at work or is unkind or unfaithful or rude and cruel. And that first impulse of anger or indignation might be appropriate, especially, the Bible tells us, when we're angry and indignant about sin and its destructive nature. Sin should always make us angry.

In a marvelous booklet, *How Can I Forgive?* by Vera Sinton, she makes this point early on. "Feeling anger when you have been hurt by someone is not wrong." She then adds: "It is a normal reaction and the sign of a healthy personality."

She suggests that, just as pain is an important signal to your body that something is dangerously wrong, anger is often an appropriate warning to you that something is amiss. But then she goes on to say the same thing the Bible says: initial anger is often a good thing, a necessary thing, even a righteous thing. Even Jesus had things happen to Him, which caused—at that moment—good anger. But here's part two of the diagnosis. Continued anger, nonstop anger, "grudge" anger . . . that's a different thing. That is harmful. And dangerous. And it puts you on a road that leads to sin.

We really ought to read the entire Bible verse, which is always a good idea. Here's Ephesians 4:26 again, and please take note: " 'In your anger do not sin.' " So far so good. But as we continue: "Do not let the sun go down while you are still angry." And verse 27: "And do not give the devil a foothold."

I appreciate how the Clear Word paraphrase interprets this Bible passage, because it speaks directly to the issue of resentment. "If you get upset, don't focus on your feelings until they become hateful and degenerate into sin. Be angry with sin, but don't sin by being angry with the sinner." Then Paul adds in verse 27: "Determine to get over any anger before nightfall, or the devil will gain a foothold."

In her routines, comedienne Phyllis Diller was always duking it out with her moron husband, Fang. "Never go to bed mad," she advises. "Stay up and fight!" But in a sense, she's right. It's better to stay up and throw pillows for a while, to stay up and fight, than it is to harbor a grudge, to stay mad overnight, or over a month or a year or a lifetime.

So the Bible's "sunset clause" is good counsel, even though it's painfully hard—and we might well ask a huge, universal HOW right here. HOW do we keep from focusing on our hatred? That stupid boss is right in front of us every single day, Monday through Friday, plus we get his obsessive, trivia-packed faxes all weekend! How can we put away our anger when the sun goes down, if the red-hot feelings don't go down as well?

How Long Should You Hold a Hand Grenade?

Philip Yancey shares another word about "imprecations," this reference from Miroslav Volf and the book, *Exclusion and Embrace:* "For the followers of the crucified Messiah, the main message of the imprecatory Psalms"—that's the sock-'em-in-the-jaw kind—"is this: rage belongs before God. This is no mere cathartic discharge of pent up aggression before the Almighty who ought to care. Much more significantly, by placing unattended rage before God we place both our unjust enemy and our own vengeful self face to face with a God who loves and does justice."

That's powerful, isn't it? Maybe we could say that even good anger is like a hand grenade that gets unexpectedly tossed in your lap. That's not your fault. That's not wrong. But the fuse is ticking. Give it up quickly, before sundown tonight, to the divine demolition team.

CHAPTER

Capital Punishment— and a Little Bit More

If you could attach a bar code, or a sticker price, to your favorite grudge, your most cherished hatred, how much would it be? What would it cost, in dollars and cents, to make it worth surrendering? The amazing reality is that you cannot ever really get even. You can't collect in full.

Have you ever thought to yourself, "So-and-so has really hurt me, really stuck it to me. But if I can do 'X' to him back, that will even the score"? And "X" was either some dirty deed in return, or some marvelously fiery, eloquent, razor-sharp speech, delivered in front of not only your enemy but about 150,000 cheering supporters, or some equally ideal penalty. The absolutely perfect punishment, tailor-made by you—with many hours of careful thought put into it. Does this ring a bell? I think I can hear a whole choir of bells going off at this very moment. We've all done this. It's called nursing a grudge, and quite a few of us have R.N. degrees—in fact, we have M.D.s and Ph.D.s in grudge-nursing.

Perhaps you remember a classic old line from the 1973 comedy caper entitled *The Sting.* It won the Best Picture Academy

16

Award that year, and maybe audiences liked it so much because this was essentially a story about seeking revenge. The crooked New York banker, Doyle Lonigan, had ordered a couple of his thugs to get rid of a Chicago con artist named Luther. And the entire film then revolves around a plot where Luther's partner, Robert Redford, and Paul Newman try to get revenge by conning this Lonigan out of half a million bucks on a fake horse-racing scheme.

At the very end of the adventure, they do indeed sucker Mr. Lonigan out of his suitcase full of cash. And Newman turns to Redford and asks him: "Well? Is it enough?" In other words, is this bucket of cash enough to make up for your friend Luther being killed? Has vengeance been satisfied? Are you happy now?

And Redford slowly shakes his head. "No," he says finally. "It's not enough." Then he laughs. "But it's close. It's real close."

That line before the final credits in *The Sting* really says a lot to us about our desires for revenge. The bottom line is that you can't get there. You may get close, but no way can you balance the scales. You can't really get even. There is no "there" there, as the old saying goes.

In his book, *What's So Amazing About Grace?* Philip Yancey has a chapter entitled "Getting Even." Some of the stories he shares leave you reeling; they absolutely do. But about halfway through, he includes a line from the great writer, Lewis Smedes. "Vengeance is a passion to get even. It is a hot desire to give back as much pain as someone gave you."

Isn't that it right there? You give me 50,000 volts; I want to give you 50,000 volts. You cause me "X" amount of hurt or shame; and I won't sleep at night until I've come up with a plan to pay you back right up to the ounce. But Smedes tells us how futile this is. "The problem with revenge is that it never gets what it wants; it never evens the score. Fairness never comes.

The chain reaction set off by every act of vengeance always takes its unhindered course. It ties both the injured and the injurer to an escalator of pain. Both are stuck on the escalator as long as parity is demanded, and the escalator never stops, never lets anyone off."

And of course, the history of this planet is a blood-spattered story of how people simply cannot get off the escalator of revenge. If you want to balance the scales, you never can. You can't get "parity"; no chance. Because, of course, as soon as you even clear your throat to begin the payback process, your enemy—thinking the exact same thing about you too—starts it up again. You can't catch up. It really is like the old nuclear policy between the U.S. and the U.S.S.R.: "M.A.D." "Mutually Assured Destruction." I have so many jet fighters; you have so many jet fighters. I have this many nuclear missile silos; you have them too. Building up, building up, madder and madder and madder.

Just one page later in Yancey's book, he quotes from a theologian named Romano Guardini, who sees our entire human race on this one-way escalator: "As long as you are tangled in wrong and revenge, blow and counterblow, aggression and defense, you will be constantly drawn into fresh wrong. . . . Only forgiveness frees us from the injustice of others."

Helen Prejean, who worked both with Death Row inmates and also with the families of the victims, poses the question: What price could possibly make up for the fact that this man, this rapist, destroyed your teenage girl? He brutalized her, he terrorized her, he killed her at point-blank range. And now we ask you, the victim's mom: Would a certain dollar amount balance the scales? That's the stupidest question in the world. Would a certain number of years in prison, a really bad prison, make things right?

Capital Punishment—and a Little Bit More

How about death itself? Would "an eye for an eye, a die for a die" be enough to actually balance the scales and bring peace to a wounded heart? With amazement, Sister Helen Prejean writes that even the electric chair was not enough to fully pay back for these heinous crimes. Here's her stark testimony: "Vernon begins to cry," she writes. "He just can't get over Faith's death, he says. It happened six years ago but for him it's like yesterday, and I realize that now, with Robert Willie [the killer] dead, he doesn't have an object for his rage. He's been deprived of that, too. I know that he could watch Robert killed a thousand times and it could never assuage his grief."

And this next line is so telling. "He had walked away from the execution chamber with his rage satisfied but his heart empty. No, not even his rage satisfied, because he still wants to see Robert Willie suffer and he can't reach him anymore. He tries to make a fist and strikes out but the air flows through his fingers."

One thing is true: a story like that helps to put our own grudges into perspective. But I know that my pet hurts are still very precious to me sometimes, and yours are as well. You may not be waiting outside the gates of Death Row, eager to light off sparklers. But there's someone out there right now, most likely, and you've been waiting a long time for a fair amount of hurt to land on their head. And yet the court transcript is painfully clear: you can't get there from here. There's no pot of gold at the end of the rainbow of revenge.

The Bible doesn't say it just like that, but it does tell us not to even try to get even. "Don't take it upon yourself to repay a wrong; leave that to the Lord" (Proverbs 20:22, *The Clear Word*). And just one chapter later: "The wicked will eventually bring on themselves the suffering they have caused others, and transgressors will end up paying for what they have done to the righteous" (v. 18, *The Clear Word*).

I know as well as you do that no matter what the Word of God tries to tell us, something inside of us is going to tell us to keep scrambling up the down escalator. Even if we can't ever get to the top. Even if we can't exact perfect revenge. We'll take imperfect if we have to. We'll settle for fifty cents on the dollar if necessary. "Even if it's an unfinished journey, I'll enjoy the drive," we think to ourselves. "Boy, will I enjoy it!"

But even that isn't true. This Vernon, the broken-hearted dad in *Dead Man Walking*, found that nothing but misery accompanied the road to revenge. There was no happiness for him, even sitting in a little room at Angola at midnight, watching a man walk the "green mile" and then die in the electric chair.

And it's the same for all of us. We've all seen the results of simmering, unsettled anger. It's exacted a cost every time. It's ended badly every time. It's brought sorrow and spiritual hurt, never satisfaction. Every time.

But back to this verse in Proverbs: "Don't take it upon yourself to repay a wrong; leave that to the Lord." If a perfect payback is needed for some enemy of yours, only God can really deliver. Only God can truly punish to perfection. Only God can fix it so the scales of justice balance right down to the penny. And He will. He promises that He will. In His time and in His way and with His wisdom and unstoppable might. But we've got to let Him do it. We've got to let Him show His might and keep His promises in His own way.

And that's forgiveness right there. Giving it to God and then walking away from the escalator. "Not my will, but Thine be done."

20

CHAPTER

Wound-up Anger
on *The West Wing*

For eight years he flew in Air Force Two. He stood in the shadows
while this bigger-than-life president, Bill Clinton, got all the
headlines and the applause. And then, after eight years of waiting
in the wings, Vice President Al Gore came away with . . .
absolutely nothing.

It's just about the hottest thing on American television these days, once you get past Regis Philbin's matching shirts and ties and all of these desert island survivor shows. But NBC's *The West Wing*, set right in the White House of the United States, gives us an almost achingly perfect picture of the pain caused by human jealousy and greed.

Martin Sheen plays a progressive Democrat president named Josiah Bartlet. And the interesting subplot story is about the vice president, Mr. John Hoynes, a bit-role held by Tim Matheson. And it really is a *bit* part. NBC's official Web site, where it describes the main players, doesn't have the vice president listed. On some episodes he doesn't even appear in all the action with Josh and C.J. and the others.

But here is a man consumed with jealousy toward the president. He hates him. He loathes him. He should be the one who sits at the big desk in the Oval Office. In fact, the season opener in October 2000, revealed how, back in the primaries, it was John Hoynes who, at one point, led in the polls by 40 or 45 points. Now he's under Bartlet, second in command to Bartlet, attending weddings and funerals while this man he despises runs the country. You talk about stomach-twisting pain!

We often complain, "I've Got to Nurse This Grudge Because It's SICK!" And that word "sick" is in there for a reason, because unresolved anger and resentment actually can make you sick. An old medical journal called "Holy Bible" says as much. Here's the diagnosis from the book of Proverbs, chapter 14: "A heart full of peace gives life to the body, but envy and jealousy rot the bones" (v. 30, *The Clear Word*).

When you and I walk around boiling with resentment or jealousy, when we harbor hatred and bitterness within our hearts, it actually affects the heart. It can make you sick. We've all felt the physical knots that can come when you allow a grudge to just sit there in your gut.

It's no surprise that the fictional feuds on this NBC television program find their basis in real life. Very often vice presidents have stood on the sidelines while adoring millions cheered for their boss. They've cut ribbons for little factory openings, while the main man flies to Europe and Asia aboard Air Force One.

In his two-part biography entitled *Robert Kennedy and His Times,* Arthur M. Schlesinger, Jr. describes the smoldering frustrations felt by Lyndon Baines Johnson, who had to stand aside while a young millionaire from Massachusetts, John F. Kennedy, was sworn into power. Johnson, a huge, magnetic figure in the U.S. Senate, a man used to being adored, a man used to getting his own way, now had to count the paper clips and sit quietly in meetings while JFK ran this show called Camelot.

"Every time I came into John Kennedy's office," Johnson said later, "I felt like a . . . raven hovering over his shoulder." And he hated it. He absolutely hated it. "I detested every minute of it," he confessed many years later. And "minute" turned out to be a predictive word, because his "face time" alone with the president got smaller and smaller. White House Secretary Evelyn Lincoln, who kept the logs, calculated that LBJ and Kennedy had ten hours and nineteen minutes together in private conferences in 1961. In '63 it had shrunk to just 1:53. Not even two hours together the entire year. And of course, as historians know, after the assassination and in the ensuing five years before the Los Angeles tragedy of 1968, Johnson and John Kennedy's brother, Bobby, developed a hatred for each other that was rabid, almost paranoic.

Helen Prejean describes at quite some length the "walking wounded," the victims of terrible death-penalty crimes, the moms and dads who lost children. So often the burdens of hatred and grudges were almost overwhelming. Except for the grace of God, some parents simply did not recover. "I am startled to find out," this Catholic nun writes, "that the divorce rate of couples who have lost a child is 70 percent. . . . I find out that four to seven months after the murder is a critical time for survivors because by then the shock and numbness wears off and the loss and rage set in." Then she adds: "I discover new meaning for the word 'anniversary.' "

These unresolved feelings of anger and bitterness were literally poisoning these people. They couldn't sleep, eat, relax, or play. All they could do was plot and build up and pile on and endlessly fantasize about getting even. And as it says so simply in the Bible, after a while the bones actually begin to rot.

23

The book of 1 Samuel, chapter 25, tells about a crabby, resentful man named Nabal, who, ironically, ought to be more cheerful, considering he's rather well-to-do. But he has the habit of just snapping at everyone. Like Scrooge in *A Christmas Carol,* he goes around singing: "I hate people." And when the warrior, David, who has quietly protected Nabal's turf and his flocks and herds without payment for a long time, sends a delegation at shearing time to ask him for some victuals and a few jugs of grape juice, this sour-faced man snaps at them and tells them to buzz off. But then Nabal's wife, the beautiful Abigail, intervenes and sends a huge caravan of provisions and treats to David and his 600 men, preventing a bloodbath.

Here's the kicker to the story, though. Nabal gets drunk at a party, and when his wife tells him what she's done, how she's undone his feud with her backdoor gift, he actually has a conniption fit. That's right. "He became like a stone" (v. 37), says the NIV Bible. And speaking of stones, we read that his heart fails him, he has a stroke, and ten days later this guy is stone-cold dead. It reminds me of a quote coming from our "second Bible" at The Voice of Prophecy: the *Reader's Digest!* Back in the November 1999 issue, the "Quotable Quotes" gave us this one by Jim Scancarelli: "A sharp tongue sometimes cuts its own throat."

Vera Sinton's book, *How Can I Forgive?* contains a mountain of quiet wisdom in its 48 pages. And this observation goes directly to the point regarding the physical hurts caused by our grudges. "If the resentment is strong enough," she writes, "the inner stress may take its toll on the body. Every doctor knows patients whose chronic conditions are made worse by unhealed resentment inside. So initial anger may be healthy, but long-term, unhealed anger is very dangerous indeed."

Again, it's true that an initial jolt of anger might be an appropriate thing, a necessary wake-up call when something is wrong. When a selfish deed is happening, or when injustice is before your eyes. The Bible tells us that kind of anger, the first flash of it, is not a sin. But when you hold on to it, when you nurse a grudge and let it go on for four or eight years while someone else runs the country you thought it was your divine right to lead, resentment can actually become a poison, both physically and spiritually.

A Texas mom-and-pop-type company was doing quite well, creating and manufacturing religious pamphlets and other paraphernalia for church-based groups to use. They had toll-free lines, a good sales staff, and had grown to the point of having about fifty people on board. However, a problem slowly began to manifest itself within the organization. Harmony had always been the watchword there; people got along well and enjoyed the Christian atmosphere. But for some reason, one of the two VPs began to slowly pull away from the core group in a number of ways.

The first thing might have almost gone unnoticed. But he arranged a job there for his sister, Moneta. Normally the personnel department posted openings, and regular employees got first shot at upgrading their positions. But without any paperwork, this transplanted woman from Minnesota was suddenly there at a desk. Bill had just pulled strings and made an opening for her.

Less than a year later, she got a raise. Six months after that, another one. What made it even more difficult to swallow was that Moneta was habitually tardy. Others came in at 7:30; she would often show up at ten or even not until after lunch. And it seemed to be a family characteristic, because right after the Christmas break, Bill, the VP, seemed to have inherited the same no-show tendencies as his older sister. Whole days would go by where he simply wouldn't darken the door at all.

And soon there was a bit of a rumble around the coffee machine about it. "They check OUR time cards big-time—both in and out—but Moneta comes and goes as she pleases." Unfortunately, with her two raises, Older Sister got into the habit of passing things off to one of the clerks to do a fair number of her own assignments. He was a fresh-faced kid, just out of college and eager to make a good impression, so for a while he stayed late and covered some of her reports, hoping that this Bill character would notice. But it got to be more and more taken for granted, and the whispering continued.

The other vice president, a man near retirement, was taking a strictly hands-off attitude. "I can't get into it," he would say stiffly any time an employee found the courage to complain. "As long as the work gets done."

Well, Proverbs 24:19, 20 soon got to be theme texts for this beleaguered corporation. "Do not fret because of evil men or be envious of the wicked, for the evil man has no future hope, and the lamp of the wicked will be snuffed out."

Now, maybe the word "evil" is too strong to use here. But the effect on corporate morale *was* evil. People were bothered by the double standard, and it didn't take long before the whispering turned into full-throated grumbling. Ironically, it created a situation of "Loving Hatred." Some of the employees actually enjoyed it when this errant vice president helped himself to another perk or arranged another first-class upgrade for himself when he flew out to the West coast. "That just proves what we've been saying," the shipping clerks would buzz, nudging one another with an elbow as they passed along the latest bad-news headline. It was almost a cheerful kind of fretting, as their negative opinions were confirmed time and time again.

Soon these people were going to bed mad and getting up the

next morning equally frustrated. They had road rage even before they pulled out of their own garages each day.

Think about some of the other kinds of sin the enemy can trip us up with as he starts out with anger. Isn't it true that much of our resentment of another person has to do with pride—especially wounded pride? This older sister waltzed in and landed a job she didn't deserve, a job that wasn't posted. Others in the company thought they had a shot at the position. They were more qualified, they thought. And so pride was hurt. This VP and his relative got breaks the others didn't, and egos took a hit as a result.

Here's another Sin Sequel that usually follows resentment: dissatisfaction with your own role or place. So often in the New Testament the Bible speaks to Christians about how every person is needed; each person in the Body of Christ has a valued position to fill. First Corinthians 12 is explicit in teaching this. But in their anger, people who are seething with jealousy sometimes come to loathe their own status as someone else seems to illegitimately get more than their share.

Then, of course, our anger often causes us to loosen our grip on our faith relationship with Jesus. Is our God able to eventually right all wrongs? Well, yes, we think so . . . but why in the world doesn't He do so? This mess just keeps on; the politics gets worse and worse and we don't see God acting. True, that verse in Proverbs seems to assert that "the evil man has no future hope, and the lamp of the wicked will be snuffed out." But *when?* Right now Vice President Bob is skiing in the Alps while you're still out on the shipping dock putting in unpaid overtime. That person you hate seems to have a lamp that just shines brighter and brighter, fueled by all of their illegal frequent-flier miles, and God doesn't appear ready to snuff out their good times any time soon.

On a lighter note—although maybe not *that* light—it's even true that the dilemma, the sin, of ongoing anger even leads to trampling on the third Commandment. Griping and groaning can lead to cursing and swearing; it certainly did in the ladies' room of this Texas company. Good Christians, struggling as they did with this continuing soap opera of unfair labor practices, got saltier and saltier in their expressions about it all.

And of course, the sin problem is just part of it. When we continue in a pattern of anger, of constant fondling of our hurts, we actually do pay that physical price. In his fascinating book, *The Ten Challenges,* Dr. Leonard Felder, a trained clinical psychiatrist, relates resentment to the sixth Commandment, which we might think is just about first-degree homicide. He suggests, though, that heaven is also warning us of the dangers of lasting anger, which Jesus Himself speaks of.

Then Felder goes right to the psychiatrist's couch, and reveals five results of harboring this kind of trauma:

1. An ongoing problem with food, drugs, or alcohol that serves the purpose of numbing the lingering pain you carry inside.
2. A sense of holding back or being unable to relax in certain situations that remind you of the painful incident from the past.
3. A deadening of your spirit, such that you sometimes can't feel joy, experience intimacy, or cry appropriate tears because of the psychological numbing inside you.
4. Skin problems, stomach irritations, and other stress-related symptoms that may be due to the traumatic incidents from your past.
5. A tendency to want to punish or put up a wall to-

ward your children, your romantic partner, or your co-workers if they push you or act disrespectfully toward you in a manner that re-triggers your hidden pain.

That's quite a list, isn't it? And certainly the same enemy, Satan, who loves to trap us in the sin of anger, and then spin his other webs, also is pleased when we hurt physically and spiritually from living in ongoing anger. He loves the walls that we end up building between us and our friends and co-workers. It's a kind of warfare that he is endlessly building up, escalating, shaping into the tallest possible tower.

There aren't easy answers. I remember an old film title: *Men Don't Leave.* And in this company, this errant vice president had that job. He wasn't going anywhere, and his big sister was parked right there next to him. Workers either got along, or they got out. And those that survived did so by simply immersing themselves in the promises of God. They had to give this problem every week and every day, and even every hour, to the heavenly Father who promises us that ALL injustices will finally be fixed. They had to trust in an invisible Father that the lamps of the selfish and the inappropriately powerful would someday be snuffed out.

And in a strong, quiet kind of way, that was actually forgiveness. Because from a Christian perspective, forgiveness does NOT say that a person's deeds aren't wrong. Forgiveness doesn't say, "We're ignoring this." Forgiveness doesn't say, "It doesn't matter." What it does say is this: "I'm giving this problem, this on-going problem, over to my infinitely powerful God. These injustices, as they continue 'in my face,' are now given over to Him."

Martin Luther King, Jr. once observed: "Forgiveness is not just an occasional act: it is a permanent attitude."

29

So the one true solution is perhaps hard to face, but it's really the only one that holds out any promise. **Give your anger to God.** If you hold on to it, you're going to be destroyed, because grudges and resentment are a one-way escalator to ruin. You simply cannot, in your own vengeful power, balance the scales. You cannot get even.

Vera Sinton, in a later chapter entitled "The Role of Love," writes about the times our grudges are against someone that we've had a close relationship with: maybe a child or a spouse. And we actually love this person! But now that small hurt, that petty irritant has grown up to the point where it's gotten to be bigger than the love itself. "Forgiving is going to be hard and hurt us," she writes. "But we also know that in the long run it will hurt us more to lose their love."

Yes, forgiving is hard. It's an act of faith. It's a willingness to wait, while God, the righteous Judge, takes His own sweet time about balancing all the rights and wrongs of the world. But in the end, it would be a bigger hurt to lose that person you love. And even if right now you're hating someone that you actually hate, your grudge is going to cause you more hurt too.

I imagine the brilliant television scriptwriter, Aaron Sorkin, who feeds those jealous lines to this fictional VP, John Hoynes, wouldn't want him to read in the book of Proverbs: "Don't be envious of dishonest [or even honest] people who have more than you; let the Lord be the center of your life."

Yes, "Let the Lord be the center of your life." For the vice president in all of us, that's the best bumper sticker in town.

CHAPTER

World War III Over a Quart of Strawberries

A lady with her feelings hurt was thinking wild thoughts like this:
"I should sue. I should really get an attorney and just sue the socks
off that so-and-so." But she finally calmed down and realized that
suing your DMV driving instructor because you flunked the test is
probably overreacting.

It was a Navy minesweeping ship, in hostile waters at the very height of World War II. And the captain was in a dither, about to launch a full-scale investigation. Thievery was happening aboard the ship, and now the skipper was outlining his comprehensive strategy to expose the guilty party.

Well, if you're not familiar with this story, the captain's plan had four parts to it. First of all, every man on board the ship—and there were a whole lot of them—was to write out a sworn-under-oath statement about his whereabouts on the night in question, 11:00 P.M. to 3:00 A.M., have two fellow crewmen substantiate and sign the statement, and have all statements turned in by 1700 hours.

Second, because the skipper was convinced someone on board had an illegal key he had made, every single key on board the ship was to be tagged with the owner's name, and turned in to the executive officer. Third, to make sure all keys were accounted for—and Steve, the exec, was guessing there might be 2,000 of them scattered about the ship—the officers were to conduct a thorough search of this huge minesweeper: stem to stern.

Fourth, to guarantee that the offending sailor didn't have the key hidden in his shoe, every single man on board was to be strip-searched.

Does all this sound simple? Well, Executive Officer Steve Maryk didn't think it was simple. He didn't think it had a ghost of a chance of working. "Captain," he said, "even if there is such a bootleg key on board, the guy who made it will just toss it overboard. Or hide it. There are a million places on this huge ship where we couldn't find a key if we looked for fifty years."

But Lieutenant Commander Philip Francis Queeg insisted that he could find the key and that his men were to get started on Plan One, Plan Two, Plan Three, and Plan Four to uncover that key and restore the *U.S.S. Caine* to a state of law and order.

Well, it's one of the great naval tales of all time, told so compellingly by the novelist Herman Wouk. Maybe you've seen the film where Humphrey Bogart rolled his little steel balls in his hand while the typhoon struck, and then later as Barney Greenwald relentlessly exposed him as a paranoid, mentally unfit captain who deserved to be replaced during "The Caine Mutiny."

But what does this story of keys and storms and Navy Article 184 have to do with the topic of grudges and revenge? Certainly the men on board the *Caine* were simmering with hatred for the captain; they thought endlessly about ways to get rid of "Old Yellowstain," including tossing him overboard on a moonless night. And in considering the resentment of Willie Keith and Maryk and Keefer and the others, the spiritual principle for us to consider is simply this: **We often hold a grudge in some area where we are vastly overreacting to the situation.**

Humphrey Bogart was willing to turn the entire boat upside down, during a time of war, with bullets flying through the air and enemy subs lurking all around them in the dark green water. And he wanted to search for an allegedly missing key . . . because of one missing quart of strawberries.

That's it. One quart of strawberries gone. And Queeg decided someone had stolen the strawberries, so someone had to have a key, and he was going to find that key, and so, Maryk, call the men on deck and strip-search them, and scour this entire minesweeper from the boiler room to the crow's nest, and stop all of World War II to find this key because there's got to be a key . . . because a quart of strawberries is gone. A quart of strawberries.

The upshot is this: don't invest in a million-dollar grudge campaign over a fifty-cent problem. There on the *Caine*, Maryk said to Queeg as he was issuing his insane orders: "Sir, let me ask you, with due respect, is it worth doing all this to the crew for a quart of strawberries?"

Even Jesus tried to teach His followers the importance of keeping a healthy perspective about things. In His famous Sermon on the Mount, found in Matthew 5, He gives this counsel: "Why are you so picky with your brother when you probably have bigger faults than he has?" (*The Clear Word* paraphrase).

You might recall the King James metaphor about the mote, or tiny splinter, in your neighbor's eye, which you kindly volunteer to help him with . . . while there's a huge two-by-four in your own. "How do you expect to help him," Jesus asks, "when you can't even see your own mistakes?"

The *Reader's Digest* January 2000 issue had this inspired gem from Georges Courteline: "If it was necessary to tolerate in other

33

people everything one permits in oneself, life would be unbearable."

And in some of Jesus' parables, we're reminded again to bear in mind this quart of strawberries. Someone else where you work gets five talents handed to him or her, while you get only two, or maybe even just one. And Christ, in that famous parable, essentially says: "Don't worry about it. Just be faithful with the two or the one." You work the whole, hot, sweaty day for a paycheck, and someone else works just one hour—in the shadiest part of the field, and in the coolest twilight hour—and gets paid exactly as much as you. What does Jesus say? "Don't worry about it." Peter finds out that at the end of life he's going to die a martyr's death, even a death on the cross. So, of course, he pipes right up and asks Jesus, "Lord, what about John? You know the future; what's going to happen to him?" What does Jesus say? "Don't worry about it."

And that's really it. Don't worry about it! Because if you're vertical with God, if you have a saved, born-again relationship with the Savior of the universe, and are going to live a few billion years in a heavenly mansion, don't most problems here below shrink down until they're on the level of a quart of strawberries? I mean, really?

We get so angry sometimes about our dilemmas, our grudges. And then we read a book like *Dead Man Walking,* where people endured unbelievable injustices. Their own kids raped, dismembered, killed. And it helps us to keep our own resentments in perspective. Jesus is telling us here: "Friend, when you stack up all of life's hurts against the centrality of the Cross, they're going to lose their magnitude."

My daughter Karli recently headed up to Cal Poly University in San Luis Obispo. Lisa and I were delighted when she ended up being assigned with another Christian young lady.

But—as new roommates, randomly assigned roommates some-times do—there were adjustments as they tried to learn to get along, to adapt to the other person's quirks, the other person's chosen bedtimes, etc. And when Leah, kind of on her own, in-vited several friends over to the dorm room for a weekly Bible study group, and didn't consult her roommate—well, there was some tension. Strange kids in my room? Sitting on my bed? Maybe borrowing a pencil out of my desk drawer without per-mission? You should have asked first, don't you think? That kind of thing, and for a couple of days, the grudge kind of sat there between them.

Now, this was certainly a speck-of-sawdust bit of hurt, maybe just a quart, or a pint, or a spoonful of strawberries. Not worth World War III, that's for sure.

And then, just a day or two after this tiny *Caine Mutiny* skir-mish, Leah got a phone call from home. There'd been a plane crash. Two of her very good friends had been in that plane. Now one was seriously injured, the other one dead.

And just like that, the paradigm in that Cal Poly dorm room was different. A close friend was dead! Leah was grieving! Her sister in Christ—grieving! With that in mind, was it really worth it for Karli to worry about a couple of kids being in her room and mussing up the bedspread on her bed while they had a little Bible study group? Was it worth it to fight about that, when this was the time to close ranks and fight the common enemy?

Here's another word of "Scripture" from that second Bible again: *Reader's Digest,* the May 1999 issue. "The art of being wise is the art of knowing what to overlook."—William James.

Listen, friend, don't overlook the Cross. Overlook the rest.

35

A Groove in the Brain

It's sometimes called a one-note sonata, or a one-string violin. And it's the symphony of your anger, your grudge against that certain person. Sometimes we literally lose hours a day, obsessing, fixating, mentally caressing the revenge that never quite materializes.

She's taken quite a beating lately in the world of media public relations, but I have to make a confession: I do like a book co-written by a certain radio personality named Schlessinger—better known as Dr. Laura. There's a fair amount of insight to be found in this volume entitled *The Ten Commandments: The Significance of God's Laws in Everyday Life.* I wrote a radio series once, sharing some material from chapter 10, which deals with the temptation of coveting. Being discontent with the things we have, and resenting other people for the things they have.

Of course, the tendency to hold a grudge, to nurse a grudge, is part and parcel of that very temptation, so I went back to her radio archives to find an anecdote illustrating the dilemma. And Dr. Laura tells about a woman who called her radio show and confessed that she was being eaten alive with jealousy and resentment over a friend who had landed a great job.

A Groove in the Brain

Has that ever happened to you? Someone else is riding high: new job, new car, long, expensive vacation. And this person is your friend! But as you compare your pay stub with theirs, your Polaroid journal describing your trip to Fresno in a Winnebago with their digital diary about Denmark and the blue Danube . . . you begin to nurse a grudge.

And you cry out to anyone who will listen: "I've Got to Nurse This Grudge Because It's SICK!" But think about what a nurse does. He or she hovers over you—at least in the days before HMOs—paying attention to you. Are you comfortable? Can I get another pillow for you? Here's a pill to shrink your swelling or mask your pain. Here's a drink of water; here's a tray of yummy cafeteria gelatin. They make you the center of attention, the focal point of their own lives.

And when we nurse a grudge, isn't that what we do? We pay endless attention to the hurt, to the envy. We play a scene over and over in our minds, fluffing up the pillows around our pain, feeding our bruised ego all sorts of medicines so it can grow and flourish. We don't want to let our grudge check out of the hospital—oh no—but we want it to be as healthy as possible in the intensive care ward.

So we're advised to put our minds to other topics, other interests. Don't nurse a grudge and feed the hungry lions of resentment. And that's where the hard debate begins. How in the world do we change a mind when it's *our* mind?

Here's a tweaked follow-up line to that bit of country-western wisdom from Hank Williams: "I can't stop . . . HATING you. It's useless to say. So I'll just live my life in dreams of yesterday." Do you remember that part? And sometimes when we're angry, we make a conscious decision to keep focusing on that bad dream of yesterday, that negative memory. We choose to resent and to be continuously mad.

Now why? Again let's reiterate—and it seems strange to face this reality—resentment is an enjoyable thing! It's a feeling of self-righteousness, of self-pity, of self-excuse, and self is one of our favorite words. We all like a bit of pampering, even if we have to do it ourselves. Eric Hoffer, a U.S. philosopher from a few years ago, observed, tongue in cheek, in his book *The Passionate State of Mind:* "To have a grievance is to have a purpose in life!"

Somebody once noted that to keep a good feud going takes a lot of work! And sometimes we find that work almost pleasant. And yet, as we face up to what God wants us to be, as we consider the poisonous effects of long-term resentment, deep down we know we need to be set free. Especially as we try to measure how the Church is hurt, how God's missions in this world are hampered by our hatreds.

What does Dr. Laura recommend to her jealous caller? "I suggested she throw a congratulations party for her [friend,]" she writes, "or send her a congratulatory note, or something that would express the exact opposite of what her envy might lead her to do."

Would that be hard to do? Write a note of praise to that person whose triumph makes you boil over? That's a tough diagnosis, doc, and an even tougher prescription. But notice how it turns out: "Each and every time I have made this recommendation," Dr. Schlessinger writes, "the caller expressed immediate relief from the ugly burden they'd been carrying, as well as a more positive feeling. In contemplating the good deed, their minds returned to good thoughts. Not only do good thoughts usually result in good deeds, good thoughts can resurrect good thinking."

Here in chapter 5, then, this is our Goal for the Day: **Determine not to nurse your hurt.**

A Groove in the Brain

When we nurse a grudge, what is our mind filled with? Bad thoughts, of course. We rehearse and practice the angry things we'd like to say; we mentally fondle the image of that enemy getting their comeuppance. We enshrine the moment when they're defrocked, stripped of their ill-gotten glories, laid bare for the hollow jerk we know they really are. In our minds, we play with that scene, play with it, play with it. Negative thoughts, spinning around, piling on top of each other, growing from a molehill into a mountain that dwarfs Everest in its shadow. But notice this sound observation by Dr. Laura: A good deed gets your mind to return to good thoughts. What we want upstairs is good thoughts, not negative ones. We want to give that nurse her pink slip, tell her that her services are no longer required.

The great Christian writer, C. S. Lewis, spent many long years corresponding with an American woman he never once met. For nearly thirteen years, despite his busy schedule, this busy, often fatigued, and overworked scholar took time to respond in longhand, answering her spiritual questions, counseling her about temptations and grievances that were invading her soul. And she must have been a rather petty, cranky person, because his replies, published after his death in a book, *Letters to an American Lady,* often deal with this issue of nursing grudges. What should a person do when struggling with resentment that simply won't leave the brain? It won't go away! The anger doesn't die down. Apparently, "Mary" must have had a real enemy lurking in her life. And check out the diagnosis Dr. Lewis, or "Jack," as he signed these more than 100 letters, shares:

"I mustn't encourage you to go on thinking about her," he writes. "That, after all, is almost the greatest evil nasty people can do us—to become an obsession, to haunt our minds."

And his next piece of advice sounds about as wretched a prescription as Dr. Laura just wrote on her pad. "A brief prayer for them, and then away to other subjects, is the thing, if one can only stick to it."

Is this possible? Yes, Jesus prayed for His enemies . . . is it really possible that you and I would do the same? Of course, it must also be noted that Jesus endured more than we did, and He prayed for people hammering nails into His hands and feet *as the hammering was going on.* Can we pray for our enemy? The person we've been ranting and raving about—can we now pray for them?

And then notice this next challenge regarding that stuck record playing in our brains. "Away to other subjects." That is just about the hardest thing in the world to do. "Away to other subjects"? Because we've worn a groove toward this subject, not away from it. All roads lead to Rome, and Rome is where we've erected our magnificent altar of anger. Our mind naturally slides toward this cherished anger, not away from it. And yet this is what we're advised to do: "Away to other subjects."

Dr. Lewis wrote that particular letter on March 10, 1954. Sixteen pages later in the book skips us over to June 21, 1955, more than a year later, and the grudge is still in ICU, getting a lot of attention. Now he writes this: "I'm sorry about your two jealous colleagues." This next metaphor is most interesting. "I suppose the only way with thorns in the flesh (until one can get them out) is not to press on the place where they are embedded; i.e. to stop one's thoughts (firmly but gently: no good snapping at oneself, it only increases the fuss)."

Isn't that a thought-provoking illustration? You've got this thorn embedded in your arm. Or, in this case, your mind. Most of the time it really isn't that big a deal . . . a quart of strawberries. But you have that tendency to magnify it beyond reason. And then you push on it. You think about it, and obsess about it. Then it hurts.

Of course, you'd like to cut it out and toss it away, but until the time comes where you can do that, Lewis writes, just stop pressing on the spot! Stop dwelling on it! Stop nursing it! Say that quick prayer, and then force your mind away. If your mind slips back into reverse twenty seconds later, force it away again. Put some good Christian music on your CD player. Listen to *The Voice of Prophecy!* Read a chapter in the Bible. Sit down and make a list of all the good things Jesus has done for you, beginning with the C's and Calvary and going from there. But just keep moving away, moving away, moving away. I've found in my own life—not as much as I'd like, to be sure—that if we seek God's help, it certainly is possible to gently but firmly stop our thoughts from going toward that favorite grudge.

Some of us catch ourselves standing in the shower in the morning and thinking about that certain person we're upset with. Or maybe as you go for your evening walk or lumber around the three-mile track in the early morning hours. These are times when we're tempted to rehearse that same cherished but worn-out speech. It's a speech we never really give, but we just keep practicing it!

And so Lewis advises us, and the Bible advises us: "Move away from there!" Say a prayer for that person, and then direct your mind to move on! Get to another topic! As people say it these days: "Get a life!" If we do breathe a prayer, asking for God's help, and then deliberately turn our minds to another topic, the mind can be directed! "Gently but firmly," we can move to higher ground.

Of course, the same decision may need to be made again ten or fifteen minutes later! C. S. Lewis himself observes in another book that when Jesus talked to His disciples about forgiving someone 490 times, He might well have meant forgiving one person 490 times for the same one thing, the sin committed just one time. But we have to mentally keep forgiving over and over, resolutely moving the mind away from that cherished cesspool of rage again and yet again.

In her book, *Beyond Ourselves,* Catherine Marshall recommends this prayer: "Lord, You have plainly told me that all vengeance is thine, not my business at all. You have said that I must forgive. I am willing to, but I've tried over and over, and the resentments keep surging back. Now I *will* this bitterness over to You. Here—I hold it out to You in my open hand. I promise only that I will not again close my fist and reclaim the resentment. Now I ask You to take it and handle these emotions that I cannot handle."

The Bible tells us in the book of Romans, chapter 3 : *"Yes, all have sinned; all fall short of God's glorious ideal"* (v. 23, TLB). *"[We all] come short of the glory of God,"* it says in the King James. That person you resent so bitterly is without a doubt a sinner. The Bible says so. But you're one too, and so am I. The human race is one motley collection of pretty hopeless people. Maybe there are different shades of wickedness and selfishness, but I doubt if those shades matter much to God. You and your enemy both stand in the same corner of need.

So then, if it's difficult to pray for that stupid person, that unkind, insensitive man or woman, it might be well, first of all, just to stand in the shadow of the Cross for a few minutes. Try to sense how both you and he need the grace of Jesus, the covering robe of Christ's righteousness, the saving power of the blood applied for the both of you.

And then maybe we can pray for that person. In another of his letters to the American woman, C. S. Lewis made this helpful confession: "I'd sooner pray for God's mercy than for His justice on my friends, my enemies, and myself."

The scary thing is this: when you endlessly nurse a grudge,

nurse it, doctor it, fuss over it, fondle it—and that mental groove toward your anger wears deeper than any possible road away from it—it can literally warp your mind until you cannot think straight. You lose all objectivity. You begin to see phantoms: wrongs and insults where none exist.

If anybody ever had a right to harbor a grudge, Martin Luther King, Jr. would be one such person. He endured a lot of hurt in his all-too-brief life and ministry. But here's what he writes in his book, *Strength to Love*: "Like an unchecked cancer, hate corrodes the personality and eats away its vital energy. Hate destroys a man's sense of values and his objectivity. It causes him to describe the beautiful as ugly and the ugly as beautiful, and to confuse the true with the false and the false with the true."

That's scary, isn't it? Maybe you remember, how in *Les Miserables,* the character Javert stalks and chases down the hero of the story, Jean Valjean, for something like twenty years. Valjean is a criminal! He stole a loaf of bread! And just because he's now an upstanding citizen, mayor of the town, helper to so many that are down-and-out, he still belongs in a French prison, as far as Javert is concerned. He's still inmate #24601. And through the entire saga, which runs well over three hours if you've seen the musical, he can't let this grudge match go. He must get his man. He must repay his adversary.

How can we get over the fact that we actually LOVE the chase, the eternal hunt to get even, to put our enemy behind bars? In the Bible, it was Saul and David. They hated each other! Even though David was a great warrior on Saul's behalf, killing Saul's enemies, the king couldn't stand this man. He spent years tracking his adversary over hill and dale.

And it got to the point where Saul could see nothing good in David. Nothing! Just as Javert, the zealous gendarme, could not acknowledge anything about his enemy, Jean Valjean, except that he was #24601. He should be locked up. Period. No extenuating circumstances could or should be considered. And at the end of the story, when Valjean actually even saves his adversary Javert from death, the police officer just can't stand *that*. To be indebted to Valjean? Psychologically ruined by such an upside-down state of affairs, he ends his own life.

In *The Ten Challenges,* Dr. Leonard Felder writes about this tendency we all have to see our enemy as *completely* wrong. "In psychology this process of believing you are 100 percent right and the other person must be bad or evil is referred to as overidentification."

He then adds a bit more—and this comes right from his very successful practice of counseling people with these exact temptations. "It takes a conscious and deliberate effort to snap out of the trap of self-righteousness and see deeper into the humanity of the other person. It requires an almost unnatural willingness to be open to an opposing viewpoint when our more 'natural' instinct is to stick with the self-righteous idea that we are 100 percent right and the other person is either stupid, out to get us, or just 'being difficult.'"

And so often as we bounce over the potholes in our own road of life, we have this same attitude as Inspector Javert: our enemy is wrong, wrong, wrong . . . ALWAYS wrong.

Well, it's a long leap from the grandiose orchestral themes of *Les Miserables* to the twangy banjo music leading into those old *Beverly Hillbillies* reruns, but do you recall the scene? Old Uncle Jed, Mr. Clampett, discovers oil on his property. It comes out like bubblin' crude. Black gold. Texas tea. And the first thing you know, old Jed's a millionaire.

And what's the next line of advice? It even rhymes with millionaire! All the hill folks say, "Jed, move away from there!" Move away from the hills and the poverty and the possum stews that Granny used to make. Move away from the pain of poverty, and get yourself to Beverly. Hills, that is.

And this is surely the line we need today. "Move away from there!" When there's a festering wound of resentment in your life, a person whose misdeeds consume your mind, your every waking hour, this is what God's Word teaches us to do: "Move away from there!" Focus instead on the wonderful list of eight things Paul gives us in Philippians 4:8: "Things that are true, noble, right, pure, lovely, admirable, excellent, praiseworthy" (paraphrase). And how does he close? "Think about SUCH things."

Back to old Jed Clampett and that oil oozing up from the ground. In a sense, oil is a messy, gooey substance that sticks to your clothes and makes the farmland all soggy. It's like that bad spot in your relationship, where the advice, "Move away from there," is offered. But let's look at it another way. What did that oil represent for the Clampett family? Millions of dollars, of course. That's why Jed and Granny and Elly Mae and Jethro could afford to move away from there. They soon had millions of dollars in Mr. Drysdale's bank; they could afford to move away and live in a mansion.

Here's the point, and you can see it coming. You and I are millionaires, are we not? Because of the Cross, and because of the river of grace that comes bubbling out of that place we call Calvary, can't we afford to "move away from there," away from our resentments and our bits of anger? Maybe you do have a fifty-cent argument that's gone on for twenty years. You've been chasing your own Jean Valjean for a long, long time, determined to get even. But come on! It's a fifty-cent argument . . . and you're a millionaire. You don't have a banker named Drysdale; instead you have a Father who owns all the cattle on a thousand hills! You have a Savior named Jesus who made you a millionaire the minute He cried out: "It is finished!"

And right now, that millionaire status is offered to set you free, to make you well. Lewis Smedes writes: "The first and often the only person to be healed by forgiveness is the person who does the forgiving. . . . When we genuinely forgive, we set a prisoner free and then discover that the prisoner we set free . . . was us."

In *How Can I Forgive?* Vera Sinton almost makes the giving up of grudges sound harder than quitting smoking. What a powerful challenge this is: "Determine not to nurse your hurt. Don't wait for the other person; make the first move. When you talk to other people, speak lovingly of the person you have forgiven. If resentment creeps back into your thoughts, remind yourself that you have wiped the record clean—as God has done for you. The wound has been cleaned and stitched. It is healing. You are free."

CHAPTER

Ripped Off Twice

A man at the racetrack once said to a friend: "That horse owes me!" And the friend said with a shrug, "Well, then bet him again, and he can owe you twice." If you hold a grudge, and that enemy haunts your mind 24 hours a day, you're the one paying double for his meanness.

In his book, *A Man Named Dave*, Dave Pelzar points out this interesting reality: "When we forgive, we free ourselves from the bitter ties that bind us to the one who hurt us." Have you ever pondered the irony of that? Here's a person who has hurt you, wounded you. And they really have. Let's acknowledge that. In terms of the scales and balancing and all the rest, they owe you big-time. Which, of course, is why you spend so many hours thinking about revenge and curses and flat tires for them. You'd like to get even.

But now pile on the *double* irony. When they've already hurt you once, and now they're permitted to occupy your brain and steal from you maybe hours a day—and perhaps they get to do that for fifteen years—they're ripping you off twice! For the original sin, and now again because they essentially own you. If a person owns your brain, they own you.

Film critic Roger Ebert commented about a scene in the movie, *Jerry Maguire,* where Renee Zellweger and Bonnie Hunt and a whole group of women were in a kind of twelve-step program. They would sit around and complain and dialogue and role-play about how terrible their ex-husbands had been to them. And there might be therapeutic value in some such dialogues, but Ebert mentioned in his review: "Someone should tell them that resentment is simply letting someone else occupy your mind . . . rent-free."

That's true, isn't it? Rent-free. When you lose hours plotting and scheming and fantasizing about what that person did to you—and especially if your fantasizing and plotting is of the type which never fixes anything, which is generally the case—all you're doing is permitting that person to spin your engine. They've essentially got their hands on the steering wheel of your life.

In the book *Pain and Pretending,* there's an interesting twist on the New Testament teaching where Jesus told His followers how, if an enemy like those hated Roman soldiers commanded you to carry their pack for one mile, you should carry it for two. And for any person struggling with a Javert complex, a burning resentment, it sounds like the stupidest proposal in the world. Why in the world would you do that?

Ah, but notice. The author, Rich Buhler, points out that according to Roman law, that soldier had a right to order any Jew to carry his load for a mile. And for that mile—man, he OWNED you. You were at his beck and call; he had the proverbial ring in your nose.

But now what happens if you voluntarily keep right on going and carry his pack and his water bottle for a second mile? He can't make you do that! And Buhler writes: "What Jesus was essentially saying was, 'For the first mile, the soldier has you under his control; you are trapped. For the second mile, you are under your own control and are walking in complete freedom from the law. In other words, for the first mile he has you. But for the second mile, you have him. It is an act of power, responsibility, and choice, and the result is freedom.' "

I don't know how far we want to explore the metaphor of POWER through forgiveness. Although even the Bible teaches, in that famous chapter, Proverbs 24, that when you're good to your enemies, you're actually "heaping coals of fire on their heads." But it is true that whenever we seek God for the purpose of moving our minds away from our hurts and away from our resentment, freedom is the promised result.

I remember an old anecdote, which I couldn't track down regarding where it came from, though it reminds me of the late Dale Carnegie. But a certain person was maneuvering through heavy traffic . . . and everyone around him was driving like an idiot. People cut him off. People stalled their cars at red lights. Moron pedestrians dropped their grocery bags right in front of his car, etc. And a passenger in the front seat was about to have a coronary over it all. He was ready to pop a blood vessel. But the driver just calmly continued on his journey. When the apoplectic passenger finally exploded: "How can you stand it? I'm going nuts!" the man driving said very quietly: "Why should I allow all these people to dictate how I live?" In other words, why should their behaviors and actions rule me?

It's interesting that the Bible takes a similar vein on all this. In the book of Proverbs, King Solomon observes that our resentments often swallow us up instead of the other person. "A man who digs a pit for others will end up falling in himself. A man who tries to roll a stone on someone ends up with the stone rolled over him" (26:27, *The Clear Word*).

49

The same principle is enunciated in the New Testament, where Jesus taught so powerfully about forgiveness and loving your enemy. In 1 Corinthians 7, Paul actually writes about slavery . . . and this was real slavery! Men and women were indentured, sold for life because of their own poverty sometimes. And Paul basically says, "Don't worry about it. If you're a slave be content—although if you can buy your freedom, certainly, go for it."

But then he tells his readers this: "If you accepted Jesus Christ as your Savior while you were a slave, the moment you did this, your spirit was set free! . . . Christ paid the price for each of you to be free. Don't think of yourself as a slave" (vs. 22, 23, *The Clear Word*).

The *Message* paraphase puts it this way: "Under your new Master [Jesus] you're going to experience a marvelous freedom you would never have dreamed of."

If the apostle Paul—and of course, Jesus was inspiring these wonderful words—wanted real slaves, slaves in chains, to feel free inside because the grace of Calvary was in their hearts, how much more should we feel free, be set free from our grudges about someone nicking our fender in the parking lot? The Bible tells us: You have Jesus! So you're free! Don't think of yourself as a slave . . . and certainly not as a mental slave to that certain someone. Back in the Gospel of John—and this is the same *Message* paraphrase, an incredible gift to the Body of Christ—Jesus says it in these words: "So if the Son sets you free, you are free through and through" (8:36). "Ye shall be free indeed," is how you might remember the King James.

Again, you and I might have to tell our minds many, many times: "Move away from there! Move away from that swamp of sinful resentment! Jesus has rescued us from there!" And now we can add this extra motivation: We just plain and simple don't

50

want that particular person out there to own us any longer. Jesus owns us, not them! Our minds belong to Him, not them! In fact, in that 1 Corinthians chapter where Paul talks about us being free, even if we have chains, he then adds: "You'll experience a delightful 'enslavement to God' you would never have dreamed of."

I think with real regret about hours and even days and weeks and months that I've lost to the enslavement of a grudge. I let someone else run my mind, occupy it, fill it up . . . and without giving me a dime's worth of rent. And all for what? The *New York Times* had a quote by Malachy McCourt, passed along in the *Reader's Digest,* November 1998 issue, courtesy of an Alex Witchel. This really hurts: "Resentment is like taking poison and waiting for the other person to die."

That is such a stinger! And the sobering, wonderful reality is that Jesus Christ wants to release us from that death sentence. "I want you to have freedom," He tells us. "I want to give you rest, give you respite from that huge, poisonous burden of the grudge you bear."

"Let's Pretend You Didn't Sin"

Is forgiveness the "doormat" experience of all time, where your enemy gets away with slapping you in the face? We sometimes feel like the forgiveness we give minimizes the reality of the crime—almost like we're saying, "It doesn't matter." Is forgiving actually a form of enabling?

They may be two of the most gripping crime-story books ever written—and the irony is that both of them were penned by a twenty-year-old, mountain-mama girl named Joy Swift. She tells her wrenching personal story in the Christian bestseller, *They're All Dead, Aren't They?* A few years later she retold the story in a more secular style for a broader audience; that book was entitled *A Cry for Justice.*

In a nutshell, Joy was only fifteen when she married an older man named George, and inherited his three kids. The teen bride immediately had two baby girls of her own, and was soon "playing house," so to speak, in a blended family of seven. George's oldest daughter, Stephanie, was just two years younger than Joy was, but she managed to be a good step-mom, a maternal authority figure to the girl and the other four kids in the house.

"Let's Pretend You Didn't Sin"

And then, one September night in 1977, while she and George were out at an American Legion community bingo game, there was the sound of police sirens. They drove home to find the hillside bathed in the flashing red strobe lights of police cars and the yellow tape marking out a quadruple homicide. All four of the younger kids had been shot dead, butchered right there in the house. The entire state of Missouri called it the crime of the century. And it stunned that Lake Ozark community when the killer turned out to be none other than the fourteen-year-old neighbor kid, Billy Dyer. For some crazy reason, he'd just gone nuts, employing a slow-witted, twenty-two-year-old friend named Ray to help him as he slipped over to the Swift home and mowed down the two boys, and two infant baby daughters, Stacy and Tonya.

The story is powerfully told about how this young mother, just twenty years old, had to cope with her grief and her anger. Being a mom was her life! It was everything to her—George and the kids. And just like that, they were gone. The ongoing rage she felt toward the two guilty murderers was a huge demon inside of her. And in the pages of these two books, she writes openly about her hatred, her thirst for revenge.

"As much as I wanted justice, I really didn't want the killer and his accomplice to get the death penalty. My reasoning behind this confused even me, since at the police station I would have gladly killed them, given a chance. Now I wasn't so sure. . . ."

Joy Swift went through a kind of religious experience during this time, so concepts of God and forgiveness began to get thrown at her, but she couldn't cope with it very well. "Someday they would stand before God," she continues, "but for now I wanted them to suffer and feel pain. I wanted them to experience a living hell on earth. I wanted them to know fear in prison, fear without escape, like my kids had felt. I wanted no mercy, for

53

they had shown none. I lay in bed at night wondering what they were doing in their jail cells. I dreamed up ways to get in to see them. 'Give me five minutes alone,' I would say. 'I just want to talk to them.'"

And this fantasy, this almost bloodthirsting dream, was one she played with over and over. Daytime and nighttime. She kept this picture of getting even in her mind 24 hours a day. "When the guard was out of sight, I'd pull a long heavy chain out from under my shirt. I'd whip them mercilessly as they cowered against the bunks. I'd make them beg the way Tonya begged, but I wouldn't stop. I envisioned gangs of prisoners surrounding them and no one hearing their cries. I wanted them thrown into a dark, windowless cell. I never wanted them to see the sun shine again. But I didn't want them dead. Not yet. . . ."

And this pattern was in her life for years. In fact, it was more than in her life; it WAS her life. It was her identifying trait. Joy Swift was the avenging angel—and there wasn't much else she WAS. She and her husband George were hell-bent on getting even with Billy Dyer and Ray Richardson.

In thinking about that radio series title, *What To Do About LOVING Hatred,* we find that this is where Joy quickly found herself. She reveled in and wallowed in her feelings of anger. She treated herself to her wounded sentiments, her hurt. She enjoyed playing out The Vision in her mind: that chain and the endless whipping of a screaming Billy Dyer. Over and over— the screams. The getting even. That bitter image became a sweet dream for her.

54

And in a thousand ways—hopefully smaller ones, but really, all hatred is poison, isn't it?—you and I have some form of this to resolve. We love to hate.

Have you ever been in a dynamic where you really did not like a certain person? For whatever reason? And maybe you had good reason not to. Your cause was just. And perhaps you soon found another person who felt the same way. Now you were really in business! The two of you could swap "stupidity" stories, exchange anecdotes, play endless rounds of "Can You Top This?" Were you enjoying your resentment, the ongoing recycle program of trading your hatred back and forth? Yes, in a wrong kind of way, you did enjoy it. But as a philosopher once observed, a good friendship cannot be based just on having a common enemy! "You hate Mr. X, and I hate Mr. X, and therein lies our friendship." That's really not going to last very long.

An old book of quotations brought this one to the surface, by the ancient writer, Juvenal: "Revenge is sweeter than life itself."

Isn't that true? I've certainly had periods in my life when I believed it was. It's so sweet to play with revenge, and plan it, and plot it, and hopefully, experience it. Ah, but examine for yourself the entire quote: "Revenge is sweeter than life itself. So think fools."

And that's really the truth in the end. Anger is such a delicious thing, but it's not a lasting sweetness. It turns on its eater, and destroys the person who hates. In both Psalms and Proverbs, the Lord gives us this plain truth. "Refrain from anger and turn from wrath" (Psalm 37:8).

Again, there's nothing sinful about some kinds of anger. God's Word wouldn't instruct us to be *slow* to anger unless there were times when it would be appropriate to *get* to the point of anger. Any Christian who didn't get angry about what happened at Columbine High School and Lake Ozark would have a problem with their spiritual thermometer. But when we have anger, it needs to be the right kind of anger, and we need to be slow getting there. Also once we get there, we need to have a spiritual way to get AWAY from anger.

That's what Joy Swift needed. That Gideon Bible she was reading said: "Turn from wrath." But how? And then: "Do not fret—it leads only to evil." Now, when your four kids have all been slaughtered, "fret" isn't exactly the right word to describe your righteous anger. But this young mother needed a way out of her rage, her helpless hunger for retribution.

There's an interesting verse in Psalm 78, and this is speaking about God, not us. But I like the picture it offers: "He prepared a path," it says, "for his anger" (v. 50).

Maybe this is what we all need. We do hate this person! And it's enjoyable; in an admittedly sinful kind of way, we savor our hatred. But deep inside, we know we're slowly destroying ourselves. We need a path for that anger, a spiritual road away from our hatred.

Joy Swift came to know what that path was. In the Christian faith, it was called forgiveness. That was her only way out. "I read it," she confesses. "I knew God meant what He said. But I wasn't ready to accept it. I wanted to shove forgiveness under a rock and walk away."

And this was a long, arduous process. Which is all right. I'm glad God is patient with me as I learn patience with others. But day by day—scratch that, year by year—Joy Swift grew in her faith. Later she writes this agonizing, but heroic admission: "I had to come to grips with the fact that Billy and Ray were also God's children, and He loved them as much as He loved my children. They had done a horrible wrong against us, but if they were truly sorry and learned from their mistakes, God could and would forgive them. That was God. And it was reasonable and fair."

It took eleven years, flashing clear down to 1988, before Mrs. Joy Swift, now a born-again Christian, made an appointment with Warden Armontrout at the Missouri State Penitentiary. She stayed overnight in a motel, praying and reading her Bible and marking verses. Matthew 5:44: " 'Love your enemies.' " Pray for them. Forgive them. And she wrote in the margin: "Billy, I forgive you."

The next day she signed in, and showed her driver's license, and went through metal detectors. And finally, after having thought about this moment for eleven years—after playing and endlessly replaying the scene in her mind—she sat in a chair next to the glass barrier and spoke over the telephone with a twenty-four-year-old man, Mr. William Dyer—the person who had shot and killed her four kids.

Point One is what she said to him that day—and this is heavy. Word for word from her book, as she reconstructs the conversation: "Billy," she said, "I came here to forgive you . . . if you're sorry for what you did. I hate what you did to my kids. I'll always hate what you did. But I want you to know that I don't hate you. You have to understand that forgiveness did not come easily for me. It's taken a long time for me to reach this point, and I don't want you to take it lightly."

Can you put yourself in that plastic visitor's chair, with the phone earpiece, and try to relate to what Joy experienced that day? What she offered? For eleven years this young woman had felt the "rot of the bones" caused by her overwhelming anger. And even in 1988 and beyond, despite her valiant efforts, bitterness and resentment were twin enemies, twin crises for Joy and her husband George. The mouth can say, "Billy, I forgive you" . . . and yet the heart can take a while to follow along. And it has taken an enormous toll on this young woman's life, the ever-present challenge of staying in an attitude of forgiveness, of giving her grievances over to God. And then again. And again. Joy would be the first to say that she dwelt in the shadow of death; she lived in the intensive care ward of the hospital of hatred for a pretty long time both before and after this prison visit to see Billy Dyer.

Those carefully chosen words Joy said in that gray-walled penitentiary give us an insightful understanding of the words that sometimes must *follow* forgiveness. Here's the message we must sometimes say to the person who has wronged us. Even as we say, "I forgive you," even as we say with our mouths and, hopefully, our hearts, "I give this to God," we sometimes need to also say this: "You are able to make choices. I hold you responsible for this action."

That's quoting directly from Vera Sinton's booklet, *How Can I Forgive?* She suggests that instead of attacking the person, we calmly address the wrong action. And express our emotions this way: "You are a mature person. You know there are things that are right and wrong in the world. You are able to make choices. I hold you responsible for this action."

It was on April 4, 1968 that a young Black minister was shot and killed. Martin Luther King, Jr., who had given his famous speech just the night before, "I have been to the mountaintop and seen the Promised Land," was dead. It fell to his friend Bobby Kennedy, speaking that evening at a political rally, to announce the assassination to a huge crowd that hadn't yet heard the news. He spoke about forgiveness and going forward together—and then was gunned down himself a few months later in Los Angeles.

Of course there was rage that evening. Millions of Americans who had pinned their hopes on Martin Luther King, Jr. turned away from their radios and television sets in horror and helplessness. What chance was there now? How could things ever improve now? They had come up with a champion, an articulate spokesman, and now he was gone. And certainly the disenfranchised populations of 1968 had to feel that raw anger;

someone out there had done this to them. THEY had done it, and now THEY should be made to pay.

But does the Bible teach not only non-violence but non-expression? When we're angry, should we only go into our prayer closets and talk to God, or should we also speak up to that person we're angry with? Is confrontation biblical?

An article by L.A. Times staff writer Beth Ann Krier points out that some people are "stuffers," who suppress anger, and many others are "escalators," which she defines as "full-out screamers and yellers." And she quotes from Dr. Hank Weisinger and his *Anger Work-Out Book,* where he warns that anger carried around for even a week is a serious problem. Anger that disturbs even one relationship is a problem. So resentment that we "stuff" can be a serious challenge, even a spiritual problem.

In his article, "Letter From Birmingham Jail," King had this to say: "Freedom is never voluntarily given by the oppressor; it must be demanded by the oppressed."

And another sound bite from that same article, later printed in the book, *Why We Can't Wait:* "We will have to repent in this generation not merely for the hateful words and actions of the bad people but for the appalling silence of the good people."

True, forgiving our neighbor and trusting in God are necessary. But there are also times when the people of God are to speak up, to protest evil, to demand repentance. In their book, *Cry of the Soul,* counselors Dr. Dan Allender and Dr. Tremper Longman make the argument that Christians are rarely angry *enough.* "The greater the injustice," they write, "the more anger we ought to feel. To read about a child paralyzed by a gang shooting and not feel angry is unholy."

So there is a time to speak up. One of the most wretched stories in the Bible actually has a decent ending, because of this very principle. Second Samuel 11 and 12 tells about a pregnant woman, a royal coverup, and Bathsheba's husband knocked off in battle as ordered by King David's signature. And it's important to notice that a number of people were in on this messy crime. David had sent for Bathsheba, so some palace servants knew. Joab, the general in the field, knew because he'd received the battle orders from David. And of course, anyone who could track a pregnancy and count up to nine months had their suspicions too. So this was a palace plot a lot of people had to be buzzing about. And talk about resentment! Was it possible that the king of all Israel was going to get away with this? Talk about high-handed! Talk about abuse of power! There had to be a real rumbling, a groundswell of frustration among the "little people" who knew what had happened.

But God doesn't stand by and expect His people to just swallow hard and choke on their resentments. He sends His own prophet, a man named Nathan, to confront His Majesty. And after a quiet little parable that makes the spiritual point he wants to convey, Nathan the prophet points a bony finger in the king's face and thunders these four words: "Thou art the man!" It's one of the great confrontations in the Bible!

So it's true that swallowing hard is sometimes the spiritual exercise we have to undergo. Sometimes when we resent a person, we're simply supposed to forgive them. In fact, we're always supposed to forgive them. But it's also true that sometimes actions and plain talking are the spiritual course to take, as Jesus did in the temple where the moneychangers were ripping people off and swiping credit cards, ATM debit accounts all over the place. He forgave sinners, yes, but on this occasion He also said a few straight words and picked up a rope for emphasis.

Back to that Martin Luther King assassination—how should those who were grieving express their anger, their resentment? Was quiet retreat the only answer? Have patience? Have faith? Put off the trip to the Promised Land for a few more decades? Certainly some patience and trust in God were in order; having faith that a heavenly Father would bring justice had to be a tough spiritual assignment for those who endured that dark April night.

But it's also good to note that exactly one week later President Lyndon Johnson went ahead and signed the Civil Rights Act. On April 11, 1968, that landmark legislation was accomplished. A great crime had been committed, but people spoke up; some legislators reacted against evil with their speeches and their ballots, and the oppressors were turned away.

Of course, speaking up in the right way is a challenge right up there with forgiveness. There are two things we all do with tremendous brilliance, of course. We're all incredibly eloquent in talking to ourselves about our anger. We so often rehearse and polish certain speeches to a Pulitzer Prize level; but we never give them to the appropriate party! C. S. Lewis, in his *Letters to an American Lady,* observes wryly: "I hope one is rewarded for all the stunning replies one thinks of one does not utter! But alas, even when we don't say them, more than we suspect comes out in our look, our manner, and our voice. An elaborately patient silence can be very provoking! We are all fallen creatures and all very hard to live with."

We often fall back, then, on the inward mutter, the ever-grinding rehearsal of our complaints. We engage in silent retribution, the "elaborately patient silence," getting back at that person with a million little psychological tactics, but not with straightforward communication.

At least we don't communicate with *that* person. It's very common, though, when we're resentful, to communicate with every other living being on the planet! Which is Strategy Number Two. And this is one of the deadliest failings in the Christian faith, when we talk to every single person we can think of about our resentment except the party in question.

A recent documentary by the National Film Board of Canada makes a powerful statement about this human dilemma. *Glimmer of Hope* chronicles the story of Don and Mary Streufert, who experienced the loss of a daughter at the hands of two young murderers. And yes, there was certainly rage—both inwardly focused and also poured out to any sympathetic ear.

But then Don and Mary and their surviving daughter Emily embarked on a project to confront these two killers. They met with both of them in prison, where they were serving life sentences. They expressed their rage—carefully, choosing words with precise judgment—but very forcefully looking at their enemies and saying to them, "This is how I feel about what you did to our family." And then right at the end of the film, they do talk about forgiveness as well, as a process now made more possible because they had communicated in the appropriate way, face to face.

The Bible has another good story on this topic of plain talk and confrontation. In Luke 19 there's a fascinating account about a vertically challenged man named Zacchaeus, who hadn't eaten his Wheaties, and decided to climb up in a sycamore tree in order to get a look at this Jesus of Nazareth. By the way, he could have afforded Wheaties—plenty of 'em—because he was a crooked tax collector, siphoning off most of the TurboTax profits for himself every time people in his territory hit the computer "send" button. On the Jerusalem 1040 forms of his day, the government was getting the 10 and he was keeping the 40.

"Let's Pretend You Didn't Sin"

But when he has an encounter with Jesus Christ, the forgiving Son of God, and becomes aware of his sin, he doesn't simply accept the gift of forgiveness. He also pledges to give back the money he's stolen; in fact, he refunds four times the amount he's looted. We don't have a transcript of what went on during that suppertime visit with Jesus, but somehow Zaccheaus came to realize that he was both forgiven *and* responsible.

When we forgive someone, we are simply taking that entire situation and giving it over to God. And it's important to notice what we are NOT doing: We are not ignoring what happened. We're not minimizing it. We're not saying it didn't happen, or that it doesn't matter. If someone breaks a vase, they broke a vase. It's broken. Forgiveness is not a huge, cosmic game of "let's pretend." In Joy's case, four kids were dead. Forgiving Billy Dyer didn't bring them back to life; it didn't imply that this horrific crime had not happened or that it didn't matter.

And we find in Jesus' own ministry that He was not simply a dispenser of cheap forgiveness. He would look right at people and say, "Woe unto you." He said to the woman caught in adultery, very gently, but also in a voice you could hear, "Neither do I condemn you. Now go and sin no more." Which was His way of clearly telling her that what she had just done was a sin. It was wrong. She did bear some responsibility. His forgiving her took away guilt, but it didn't take away reality.

Vera Sinton makes this additional point: " 'Sorry' is not a magic formula: It must never prevent us from talking about the problems in a relationship and finding real solutions."

I remember an article in my denomination's official weekly magazine, the *Adventist Review,* where a columnist suggested that someone who had been convicted of rape or some sexual crime, might, at a later time, be reinstated to employment in a position where young people were under his authority again. And there was a flood of letters from readers saying, "No, sir; I don't think so." Because forgiveness doesn't erase reality; it doesn't mean that we don't need to confront evil and say to someone, "Yes, you did this." It doesn't mean we don't have to seek real solutions, as Sinton suggests.

In a chapter entitled "When Forgiveness Seems Unjust," she tells about a London case where three men break into a house, rape the daughter, tie up the dad and the boyfriend, and beat them with a bat. This family, being Christian, offers forgiveness to the assailants. As a result, eleven months later, the judge hands down three paper-thin sentences. "The victimized family seems to be handling it well," he comments. "Their suffering must not have been too bad."

And this soft-spoken Christian victim, this dad, protests vigorously! "For him there was no contradiction between saying personally, 'I forgive them,' " Sinton writes, "and also demanding that the justice of the law be fully carried out."

In the aftermath of her prison visit, Joy Swift responded with the same quiet resolve. She looked into the dark brooding eyes of this young killer, Bill Dyer, and told him she forgave him. Because of Calvary, because of the strength of her God, she was able to say those incredible words, those liberating words. But when lawyers came to her and asked if she would give approval at his upcoming parole hearing, she gave what I think is a very Scriptural, two-word response: "No way. Not for a long, long time. No way." Release from guilt, but not release from reality.

CHAPTER

Pardoning an Unrepentant President

When you say to your rotten, dog-barking-at-midnight neighbor, "I forgive you," what does that mean? There's no Calvary involved, no hammers, no nails, no death. Why is it that when God forgives, there has to be a Cross and a river of blood?

It might very well have changed the course of U.S. history: a little TV speech entitled "Presidential Proclamation 4311." Dated September 8, 1974, it was announced by Gerald Ford, 38th President of the United States, pardoning Richard Nixon, 37th President of the United States. Invoking his presidential powers according to Article II, Section Two of the Constitution, he was forgiving Nixon for any and all offenses he might have committed against the government during the Watergate scandal.

Well, there was quite a buzz about this: a new President, after less than a month, pardoning the man who had given him his job. Ford explains very articulately, in his wonderful book, *A Time to Heal,* why he felt he simply had to do it for the sake of the nation. Ironically, as we study the biblical principles involved in forgiveness and in nursing a

65

grudge, that was precisely why he did issue the pardon.

The entire country was fixated on Watergate; America was collectively obsessing with the grudge, with a desire to "get" Nixon, to punish him, to salivate over every detail of his alleged misdeeds. What would happen to his tapes? What was on those tapes? Would Nixon do time? "We are all addicted to Watergate," Army Major Bob Barrett observed. "Some of us are mainlining; some of us are sniffing; some of us are lacing it with something else. But someone has to come along and make us, as a nation, go cold-turkey." And as it turned out, only Gerald Ford had access to Article II, Section Two. Only Gerald Ford had the constitutional authority to "forgive," to officially shut down the grudge so that the country could get on with business.

But the interesting thing is this: the whole pardon process almost came unglued before it was announced, and for one simple reason: Richard Nixon was extremely reluctant to admit he had done anything wrong. He hadn't confessed before August 9 and the famous helicopter ride forcibly whisking him away from his White House; he wasn't about to confess after August 9 either. He just did not want to say, "I was wrong."

Well, Ford's lawyers went round and round. They argued that to accept a pardon was, in and of itself, an admission that you were guilty. Why else would you need one? Just signing the paper was a tacit confession of your crime. And they cited a famous ruling, a 1915 incident known as the Burdick case, where the Supreme Court had ruled as follows: "A pardon carries an imputation of guilt, acceptance, a confession of it."

But when Ford's lawyer, Benton Becker, flew out to San Clemente to meet with the former president, press secretary

Ron Ziegler was his usual defiant, truculent self. "Let me get one thing straight," he said straight off. "President Nixon isn't signing any admission of guilt, whether Jerry Ford pardons him or not." Ford writes later how amazed and angry he was that Nixon's press secretary, Ziegler, was so unbelievably arrogant, referring to Nixon as if he were still president and calling President Ford "Jerry" like he was some errand boy. The lawyer almost turned around and went back to the airport right then and there. But cooler heads prevailed, they finally hammered out language where Nixon grudgingly admitted that, yes, he had made mistakes which many fair-minded people could construe as self-serving and even criminal, he signed the paper, Ford went on television to announce it, and the rest is history. To this day, many pundits suggest that Ford later lost the 1976 election to Jimmy Carter precisely because he issued that Proclamation, #4311.

Certainly one of the reasons why we're reluctant to forgive a person is because it seems to surrender the reality that they've done wrong! If they've done wrong, and ought to go to jail—and now they don't go to jail, it sounds like, well, maybe they didn't do the wrong thing. Maybe they didn't hurt us as bad as we've let on. Forgiveness seems to undo our moral right to be right.

In a sense, though, Ford was expressing to Nixon the words from Sinton's book, *How Can I Forgive?* "You are a mature person. You know there are things that are right and wrong in the world. You are able to make choices. I hold you responsible for this action."

Sinton continues by pointing out that forgiving someone is not at all the same as excusing them. Not the same at all: "If we excuse something that was blatantly wrong, we are saying to the offender, 'I have low expectations of you. I

67

despise you. I do not consider you worth my moral indignation.' "

She adds a sober warning that forgiveness shouldn't be used as a shortcut out of a conflict, that we have a responsibility to uphold justice in this world. But then she moves to what forgiveness, properly expressed, based in reality, can really accomplish. After you and I get up the courage to say to someone, "Yes, you were wrong, but I forgive you . . . and forgiving means that there *is* something wrong that I choose to give to the Lord rather than obsess about myself," we can then move to this point. " 'Yes, you did this thing,' " Sinton writes. "'I accept your apology. I will not hold this against you. I will trust you as I did before.' "

In a way, this all takes us into the great cosmic realm where the theological currents run very deep. What does God's forgiveness of our sins express? Instead of eternally resenting us or bearing a galactic grudge against us, God forgives us. But is His forgiveness of our sins saying that there were no sins, or that there were sins? In his book, *Mere Christianity,* C. S. Lewis has a chapter on this whole business of Calvary and the atonement. And he asks the very good question: If God wants to wipe away our guilt, why doesn't He just do it? Just because He's God? He doesn't answer to some higher court. Why a cross? Why an atoning sacrifice, this incredible gift by His own Son?"If God was prepared to let us off, why on earth did He not do so?" Lewis writes.

Well, the science of Calvary and the miracle of grace is something the redeemed children will study for a long, long time, at the feet of an Instructor who has nail scars in those feet. But part of the reason why there was an old rugged cross, and why there was blood shed on that cross surely is because sin is real. The cross is, in a very tangible way, an expression by heaven about how deadly an infection sin is. The way God forgives communicates in a manner no one in the universe can misunderstand that our sins are real. They're fatal. They're eternally destructive. And so God forgives in a way that says all of those things. He's not excusing sin, ignoring sin, covering it up, papering it over, sweeping it to the side, putting it in some closet. When He forgives through the shed blood of His own Son, He's saying to all recipients and all listeners and viewers: "I'm not ignoring sin; I'm dealing with it. I'm pardoning sin because there *is* sin to pardon."

And down here in our own hospital ward, where you and I try to decide whether to forgive someone or just keep feeding IV bottles full of nutrients to our grudges, I think Calvary provides us with an incredible model. We can forgive someone without fear that our pardon somehow erases the reality of what they did wrong. If anything, our forgiveness actually reinforces the truth of what happened. Just as Calvary is a huge, monumental, universal expression of the raw reality of our transgressions, the forgiveness we offer an offender can carry that same, quiet, moral power. In fact, it's because of the moral power of Calvary that we can forgive. "Forgive others as you have been forgiven," the Bible tells us. The Cross is a sufficient statement about evil to cover both us and those who sin against us.

Vera Sinton shares a very wise point-counterpoint discussion regarding what Party A, the forgiver, needs to do and what Party B, the "forgivee," also needs to do. "Forgiveness matched with repentance produces reconciliation," she writes. "Forgiveness is: 1) Granting free pardon for a hurt, 2) Giving up all claim for compensation, 3) Ceasing to feel resentment."

And now how does Party B, the Watergate sinner, respond?

"Repentance is: 1) Accepting a pardon for a hurt, 2) Making any appropriate restitution, and 3) Ceasing to feel guilt and shame."

Those "imprecatory psalms" found in God's Word are man's agonizing shouts to heaven, saying: "God, please clear Your throat and at least say that my enemy's sins were real, that what they did was wrong. Please!" Thankfully, Calvary says it loud and clear. For our enemies . . . and for us too.

CHAPTER

Forgiveness in a Block of Wood

There's this certain person out there that you simply cannot get along with. Past arguments have put up a ten-foot-high barrier between you, and there doesn't seem any way over, under, or around that wall of hatred. Is there any FIX at all for the kinds of simmering dysfunction we often experience with others?

It's hard to imagine this person being angry, or having a temper tantrum, but President Jimmy Carter admits that he has often struggled with feelings of ongoing resentment. Unfortunately, the person he's occasionally had an extended "Cold War" with has been named Rosalynn Carter.

Back in 1987, he and his wife decided to co-author a book, which they entitled *Everything to Gain*. It was about the 1980 election loss to Ronald Reagan, and their subsequent move back to Plains, Georgia. Unfortunately, the main thing he and she both gained was some extra blood pressure from disagreeing on how to write this stupid book. Ninety-seven percent of the time they were in perfect agreement. But on the other three percent, they almost were ready to come to blows. They didn't see eye to eye, and no amount of discussion could resolve their disputes.

Fortunately, the Secret Service was there to keep them from killing each other, but this was shaping up as a Carter catastrophe, the likes of which it was going to take the United Nations to resolve.

Finally the editor stepped in and said, "Look. In the places where you just can't agree, mark the paragraphs. We'll put it right in the book: a 'J' for yours, Mr. President, and for parts your wife wrote, we'll put an 'R' there in the margin."

And the compromise actually worked. It's the classic case of "agree to disagree," and harmony prevailed. Still, President Carter admits in his book, *Living Faith,* that there were, on a number of occasions, long silent periods of resentment between them. Hurt feelings and sulking and—dare we say it in regards to the 39th President of the United States of America—pouting? After all, he and his wife are as human as the rest of us.

And yet, this Christian man, who isn't just a world leader but also a Sunday School teacher and born-again Baptist, realized that something needed to change in his own heart. And he confessed before the entire world: "Rosalynn and I are both strong willed and frequently have disagreements, some of them lasting for several days. It is difficult for either of us to admit being at fault. Recently, after a particular disturbing argument, I decided that we should never let another day end with us angry with each other. I went to my wood shop and cut out a thin sheet of walnut, a little smaller than a bank check. I then carved on it: *Each evening, forever, this is good for an apology—or forgiveness—as you desire. Jimmy.*"

Isn't that a tremendous gift? Every evening, that little piece of wood guarantees that harmony will prevail: either with an apology or an offer of forgiveness. Whichever is needed. Carter adds this final P.S. "So far, I have been able to honor it each time Rosalynn has presented it to me. And she has!"

Forgiveness in a Block of Wood

There are a couple of points to notice. First of all, sometimes our anger can be wiped away by a simple plan. A small irritant can be erased by just putting a fix in place. Those initials by the prickly paragraphs—that took care of it. A despairing mom once wrote to a parenting specialist, beside herself over the fact that her little kid spilled the milk day after day, meal after meal. This was a case of: "Got milk?" "Nope, it's on the floor again." And the child guidance expert countered with: "Why don't you just move that glass of milk farther away from the edge of the table?" "Oh. Never thought of that." Problem solved. And many of the things that cause our resentment are just that easy.

But then Carter's second story takes us a bit deeper into spiritual realms. Because this married couple did two things. First of all, they were willing to discuss the dilemma. He acknowledged the pain these periods of emotional separation were causing. He admitted the wrongness of sulking, of harbored anger. So that's one key: being willing to talk about it. And then Jimmy Carter simply rose above his feelings and his emotions. "Every night," he pledged, "I'm willing to confess if I've been wrong. I'm willing to forgive if *you've* been wrong. But never again are we going to go to bed mad." President and Mrs. Carter pledged that because of their love, and according to their faith, they simply WOULD forgive. Every place, every time, under every conceivable and unforeseen circumstance. That was part of being a married Christian couple. That was obedience, and no matter how they felt, or if they were still convinced of the rightness of their cause, they *would* obey Ephesians 4:26, the Bible verse about not letting the sun go down while you're still mad.

Sometimes if we're looking for just a straightforward plan to end anger, it comes down to the most basic thing: an apology. In his delightful baseball book, *Field of Hope,* Brett Butler describes what it was like to play with Andre Thornton, one of the great Christian ballplayers of all time. Butler, also a Christian, considered Thornton to be a giant as a man of God. Players would be sitting around with their beer cans and their R-rated stories and their expletive-laced insults, and then Thornton would walk into the room. *Instantly* things would quiet down. Even the wildest-partying guy knew that Thornton was a Christian gentleman. And he had the home run muscle and RBI stats to back it all up.

In this little anecdote, though, Butler lost his cool once on the team plane when he spilled a Coke all over himself. And Thornton, not in his usual character, made the tiniest teasing remark. No big deal. And somehow, Brett Butler, Christian that he was, lost his cool, shouted at Thornton to shut up, and added a couple of "blank, blank, blanks." And the whole plane just cracked up. "Butler said a bad word! Butler said a bad word!" Which, with Brett also trying to be a Christian, was a big headline. Guys were high-fiving themselves with delight over this very public sin.

Obviously, Butler felt terrible about the whole thing. It ate at him all that night. And the next day he was determined to tell Andre Thornton how sorry he was. Lo and behold, before he could get a single word out, Thornton came to *him.* "Brett, I'm sorry," he said. And Butler couldn't believe it. "*You're* sorry? What are you talking about? I'm the one who lost it!" "No," Thornton told him, "If I hadn't provoked you, you wouldn't have said what you said. It's all my fault."

Brett Butler, thinking about it later, was just awestruck with this man's humility. He knew he was in the wrong. And yet, this other ballplayer was taking the blame on himself, accepting it, seeking forgiveness so that there wouldn't be even one shred of this kind of resentment, which can destroy a Christian's witness.

These two ballplayers might have just stumbled onto something regarding this issue of anger and resentment. They moved beyond anger for one simple reason: their Christian faith required it. In a sense, they didn't have any other option. Christians *must* forgive. Christians *must* reconcile.

In *What's So Amazing About Grace?* Yancey shares yet another story along these lines: "Walter Wink tells of two peacemakers who visited a group of Polish Christians ten years after the end of World War II. 'Would you be willing to meet with other Christians from West Germany?' the peacemakers asked. 'They want to ask forgiveness for what Germany did to Poland during the war and to begin to build a new relationship.' At first there was silence. Then one Pole spoke up. 'What you are asking is impossible! Each stone of Warsaw is soaked in Polish blood! We cannot forgive!'"

Over and over, this question threads its way through the topic of grudges. Are some sins just plain TOO big? Here's the rest of the story: "Before the group parted, however, they said the Lord's Prayer together. When they reached the words 'forgive us our sins as we forgive . . .' everyone stopped praying. Tension swelled in the room. The Pole who had spoken so vehemently said, 'I must say yes to you. I could no more pray the 'Our Father,' I could no longer call myself a Christian, if I refuse to forgive. Humanly speaking, I cannot do it, but God will give us His strength!'" Then Yancey adds: "Eighteen months later the Polish and West German Christians met together in Vienna, establishing friendships that continue to this day."

That's where the Christian faith takes us. Oh, there are methods and systems; we might carve out our peace pledge on a little piece of wood. Or just move the glass of milk. These days you can email an apology if you're not ready for a face-to-face. But the person who puts his faith in God is armed with the knowledge that everything God commands, He also provides for. Philippians 4:13: "I can do all things through Christ who strengthens me" (NKJV).

Benedictine monks, Yancey writes, have this ritual that helps them through the seeming impossibility of this. People with issues to resolve and pent-up anger to release gather together to share and pray. And then, even though it seems so hard, they all put their hands into a large crystal bowl filled with water, still mentally holding onto that grievance, that pain. And as they keep praying for the miracle of grace, of forgiveness, they slowly and symbolically open up their hands. And the hurt, all the built-up frustration, that long LIST they've carried with them, is slowly let go. They release it into the water of grace.

"Imagine," he writes, "what impact might it have if blacks and whites in South Africa—or in the United States of America—plunged their hands repeatedly into a common bowl of forgiveness?"

10

Forgive
Our Dust

*What did you have for breakfast yesterday morning? You probably
don't remember. What were the exact words, the rotten, stupid
words, your enemy used in that nasty speech against you back in
1983? You probably have them ingrained in your brain, word for
ugly word.*

The Red Cross's Clara Barton suffered a great injustice once.
A certain person had been unbelievably cruel and unfair to her.
Years later, though, when a friend of hers began to stoke up the
fires again, reminding her about the grievous sin, our heroine
claimed that she couldn't remember it at all. "I'm sorry," she
said, shaking her head, "I just . . . I don't recall."

"Oh, come on," the friend protested, eager to enjoy the flash
of verbal swords, eager to pull the scab off and see some fresh
blood on the floor. "It was horrible! You've got to remember
that!"

And the reply came back with quiet force. "No," she said. "I
distinctly remember forgetting that."

Isn't that marvelous? It reminds us of the classic song loved
by both Christians and Jews, found in the 103rd Psalm by King

David: "He will not always accuse, nor will he harbor his anger forever; he does not treat us as our sins deserve or repay us according to our iniquities. For as high as the heavens are above the earth, so great is his love for those who fear him; as far as the east is from the west, so far has he removed our transgressions from us" (vs. 9-12).

I love that powerful metaphor of God taking our sins, and deliberately—with that omnipotent mind of His—forgetting them. He blanks them out. John 5:24 tells us that when a person comes to God, he or she " '[crosses] over' "; they have, at that very moment, eternal life. Their sins are gone. God takes them as far away as the east is from the west.

In his book, *The Bible Jesus Read,* Philip Yancey delves into some of the fascinating Old Testament passages that have baffled Christians for centuries. And in commenting about Psalm 103, he expounds upon an Egyptian word: *Hapiru.* That's what the Egyptian masters called their Hebrew slaves: *Hapiru,* "the dusty ones." And of course, the very next two verses in Psalm 103 go like this: "As a father has compassion on his children, so the Lord has compassion on those who fear him; for he knows how we are formed, he remembers that we are dust."

And Yancey comments: "We have a God who consciously forgets our sins and consciously remembers our frailty."

How's that for a blueprint? Of course, most of the time we do it exactly opposite from that. We consciously remember— we deliberately focus on—our neighbor's misdeeds toward us. We don't consciously forget them; we consciously and carefully and methodically chisel them into the marble fresco of our mind. We rehearse them, we write poems about them, we enthusiastically relate them to our friends and relatives and even to the wrong-number telephone callers who get us out of our easy chair during Monday Night Football.

And we certainly ignore God's pattern on the second half of that equation too, where the Bible says, "He remembers that we are dust." We, on the other hand, consciously ignore the other person's frailty. We give no points whatsoever for dust or cobwebs, or background, or lack of education, or our enemy's private hurts and sorrows. The phrase, "extenuating circumstances," is totally foreign to us. Except applied to ourselves, naturally.

Dale Carnegie tells the story about how Mary Todd Lincoln, wife of our 16th president here in the United States, used to rant and rave and almost foam at the mouth about those people in the South. How could people hold slaves? How could anybody be so backward? She nursed her grievances until Lincoln must have almost wanted to leave her alone in the Lincoln Bedroom and go sleep on a couch down the hall. But, as Carnegie tells the story, President Lincoln finally said to her, very calmly, "Dear . . . don't criticize them. They are just what we would be under similar circumstances." In other words: dust. Dust born and bred in the Deep South, where plantations and slave chains and segregated Sunday Schools were how little boys and girls had been brought up for generations. They had grown up in dust, and dust is what they were. That didn't excuse evil, but it did help a person to understand why evil was there.

We're reminded right away—and it's ironic that King David is involved in this story too—of that famous verse where Samuel is looking for a new king for Israel, and God says to His prophet: " 'The Lord does not look at the things man looks at. Man looks at the outward appearance, but the Lord looks at the heart' " (1 Samuel 16:7).

Certainly you can take that verse two ways. Sometimes a person can wipe away the dust on the outside, leaving a smooth and shiny surface . . . and the Lord looks into the heart and sees the evil there, the hidden dirt. But our loving God is also able to see past our mistakes, the thin veneer of our shortcomings, and see the hardships, the frailties that we're battling. And before you and I are tempted to nurse a grudge, to remember past hurts and forget the dusty deficiencies that led to those hurts, let's try to think with the mind of Christ.

Here's yet another slice of correspondence from C. S. Lewis to that "American lady." She was a grudge-keeper par excellence; she had a mountain of resentments that piled up higher than the Statue of Liberty. We don't get to read her letters to Lewis— probably a good thing—but it's clear that she was mad just about all of the time. But he responds to one of her diatribes about a certain So-and-So: "Their penitence may no doubt be very imperfect and their motives very mixed," he writes. "But so are all our repentances and all our motives. Accept theirs as you hope God will accept yours." Then he adds this reminder, found in Matthew 6:15: "Remember that He has promised to forgive you as, and only as, you forgive them."

Apparently, unless we learn to adopt this "dust" philosophy that heaven has toward us—"God consciously forgets our sins and consciously remembers our frailty"—and apply it to those who wrong us, we ourselves might move out from the shadow of God's gracious amnesia.

A bit later in this same letter to the unforgiving American lady, Lewis adds this second thought: "Try not to think—much less speak—of their sins. One's own are a much more profitable theme! And if, on consideration, one can find no faults on one's own side, then cry for mercy: for this must be a most dangerous delusion."

Well, God doesn't have delusions . . . but you and I certainly do, don't we? It's wonderful news that God, who knows so much more than we do, is still the One who takes our trespasses and deposits them in the farthest corner of the universe, out of His own sight. It's the God, who never forgets, who deliberately *does* forget.

For us the challenge is to do the same: to deliberately, and intentionally, forget. To put out of our mind that grievance, that old hurt. And then say to our mind, perhaps many times a day, "I'm done with that! Mind, move away from there!" We need to make forgetting a spiritual principle, just as Jesus did when the nails were going into His hands and feet. How could He possibly forget, when every blow was exquisite agony? And then that whole Friday afternoon, every breath He took, every moment He endured, was pain beyond description. How could He forget then? But that's exactly what He did. "Father, let's forgive them," He said. "Even as this is happening, let's choose to forget."

Two years after C. S. Lewis sent that letter across the stormy Atlantic, he had occasion to write his friend again. He was tired and frail now; his own death was just five months away. But again, June 25, 1963, he is compelled to remind this woman of the power of forgetting, of forgiving. "I hope, now that you know you are forgiven," he writes, "you will spend most of your remaining strength in forgiving."

And it takes strength, doesn't it? It's hard to purposely forget the very things your soul cries out to catalogue and chronicle, to grip so tightly with the muscles of your mind. But notice how we can do it: "Lay all the old resentments down," Lewis writes, in the handwriting of a weary but faithful veteran, "at the wounded feet of Christ."

Yelling
at Blind People

If someone cuts you off in traffic, you get mad. Right? We all do.
But if you find out they had lost a tire, or their steering suddenly
froze up, making their car lurch in front of you—especially if they
ended up being badly injured—well, you cut them some slack.

Motivational writer Stephen Covey tells about a man on a subway who watched in frustration as another passenger just let his kids run wild. They were climbing up and over the seats, bothering other passengers, making noise, bickering and horse-playing around until you could read annoyance on a lot of faces. And finally this guy cleared his throat and said to the laid-back father: "Look, fella, why don't you crack your whip a bit and do your job? Your kids are a giant pain. Are you blind or what?" Words to that effect.

And if you remember Covey's story, the dad looked up at his accuser with anguish in his eyes. "You're right," he said, hesitantly. "I guess I should do something. But we just came from my wife's funeral. The kids just lost their mom. And I guess they're just . . . not themselves. I'm sorry."

You can imagine the long, embarrassed pause . . . with the

clickety-clack of the subway wheels reminding everyone listening in that subway car that we don't always know the whole story. There are pages hidden from our view, and funerals we don't know about.

Have you ever launched into a mini-grudge, or maybe even a maxi-one—only to find out that you didn't know about something? You go in to work, and the same guy who's late every single day is missing again. And everybody shakes their head. Some people! How does he get away with it? But then, around ten in the morning, the word begins to quietly slip its way down the halls and corridors: "Tom's wife was killed in a car crash last night."

Until that moment you were so mad. But all at once, in the famous words of *Saturday Night Live*'s Miss Emily Litella, you say: "Oh . . . never mind." And the great speech you had constructed in your mind just kind of dies right there.

In our blindness we often nurture grudges. We're mad and resentful because we don't know all the facts. But try going at it from the other side of that subway car. How often are we improperly mad at that other person because we don't take into account their blindness?

Question: You're standing on that same crowded New York subway, eagerly riding to a World Series game. All of a sudden, someone really tromps on your foot. They mash it . . . but good. *Yow!* And you whirl around to scream at them: "What's the matter with you? Are you blind?" Just then you notice their dark glasses, their white cane. And that attack line dies in your throat. "Are you blind?" Yes, they are blind. And of course, we don't get angry at a blind person for stepping on our toes; they can't help it. They didn't do it intentionally.

Vera Sinton tells a story with a pretty familiar tag line: "In 1987," she writes, "millions of viewers watched television interviews with Gordon Wilson. He and his daughter were buried in rubble by a bomb blast at a public parade in Northern Ireland. He was holding her hand as she died."

Northern Ireland has been the scene of simmering frustration for long decades now. We've all seen the CNN reports of those bomb blasts, the endless terrorism going on between the IRA's Sinn Féin organization and the Orangemen, Catholics against Protestants. And this Gordon Wilson had just lost a daughter to the violence, to "The Troubles." But notice his response, as Sinton tells the story: "He was holding her hand as she died. But he refused to nurse ill will against the bombers. 'I shall pray for them tonight and every night. God forgive them, for they don't know what they do.'"

I know you've heard that line before, and so have I. "God forgive them, for they don't know what they do." "I choose not to be angry, because the person who just stepped on my foot was a blind person. I choose not to hold a grudge because the person who lied about me was confused and mixed-up and scared, feeling so inadequate. I choose not to retaliate for this bombing, because the people who lit the fuse were spiritually blind, morally impoverished, by the accumulated effect of a million small hurts I don't know anything about."

Now it's true—there is a limit to this. There's blindness, and there's also evil. It's painfully true that people sometimes set off bombs, and they know exactly what they do. They drive nails into an innocent Savior's hands, and they do it with their eyes wide open. But how sobering to see that Jesus Christ, who was receiving those hammer blows, gave the Roman soldiers the benefit of the doubt. "Father, forgive them," He prayed. "They're blind. They don't know what they're doing. They don't realize the ramifications of this moment."

Think about that person you resent the most in life, the person you really think has abused you and abused their position and abused their power. And maybe they have. But do you know their entire background, the full history of their childhood, their teenage years? Do you know how they were raised? Do you know the private, hidden torments they've been through, the breakups they had in college, the divorces? You don't, do you? I don't either. And even Jesus, who did know what His enemies had been through, who did have a full picture of their blind spots and also their deliberate sins, chose to cut some slack for these misguided, stupid, human men with their hammers and their nails.

Here's yet another storm-tossed illustration from aboard the deck of the *Caine*. That psychotic ship captain, Queeg, made life pure hell for the officers and crew. Pretty soon they all hated him; they had grudges that were as red-hot as the mortar shells flying overhead. But author Herman Wouk describes a scene where the central character, Willie Keith, would go out on the deck and just look at the surging ocean, the vast expanse of sky. "He could, at least for a while," the author writes, "reduce Queeg to a sickly well-meaning man struggling with a job beyond his powers."

There's another pivotal scene where Steve Maryk, the executive officer, and Keefer, the ship's communications officer, go over to the Fifth Fleet to tell Admiral Halsey that their captain is a loony, and that he ought to be replaced under Navy Article 184. In fact, Maryk has a log he's kept, chronicling all of the dumb, paranoid, schizoid things the captain has done. And when Keefer begins to rant again about Queeg, about what a tyrant he is, what an abusive, evil officer he is, Maryk shuts him up with his own argument. "That's beside the point, Tom. If the old man's sick in the head there's nothing to be sore about."

And Keefer, after a long pause, reluctantly nods. "True enough." It's like a blind person stepping on your foot. It hurts, but you don't get mad about it.

In his chapter, "Nice People or New Men," out of the Christian classic, *Mere Christianity,* C. S. Lewis addresses a Captain Queeg-type problem that bothers a lot of people. And it's this: why are so many Christians jerks? Why do Christians mash your foot on the subway? Why are they so judgmental? Why are they so unfriendly in church? Why do some of them who live in Northern Ireland light fuses to bombs and kill innocent children? Why do Christians here in the United States, men who have been baptized in the tank on a Sunday morning, go out at midnight in a pickup truck and torch a Black church? Why aren't these so-called New Men and New Women very nice people? And why shouldn't I hold a grudge against a person who acts that way?

Well, Lewis acknowledges the reality that when we Christians behave badly, we make Christianity unbelievable to the watching world. But at the very end of the chapter, he gives us this quiet reminder, and really, it comes right from the foot of the Cross, where Jesus whispers those words about blindness and forgiveness. "What can you ever really know about other people's souls—of their temptations, their opportunities, their struggles? One soul in the whole creation you do know: and it is the only one whose fate is placed in your hands. If there is a God, you are, in a sense, alone with Him."

Perhaps we should all put ourselves on the deck of that ship, the *Caine.* Everywhere around us are hurting, confused, paranoid, battle-scarred people: stepping on our toes, hurting our feelings, issuing stupid orders. Some soldiers are hurting in the head; some are just plain bad. How can we know the difference? How can we decide who to nurse a grudge against? How can we decide whether to mutiny or stay with the ship? It's hard, isn't it? But all around you is the surging power of the ocean, the forgiveness of Calvary, the tenderness of the Savior who says, "Father, forgive them all; they don't know what they're doing."

CHAPTER 12

Always Mad
at Mr. Oblivious

Even if your brain-power time was just minimum wage—say five
bucks an hour—and you spend five hours each week mulling over
your hatred of that certain someone, that enemy is costing you
twenty-five dollars a week! He's using you! And he or she may not
even know how mad you are.

It's one of the most chilling profiles ever penned: a tragic story about a kid named Lee. As best-selling author William Manchester tells it, this young man had zero going for him. He was kind of short, with already thinning hair. He had a squeaky, pre-pubescent voice. He couldn't hold down a job making more than about a buck an hour back in the 1960s.

He had a wife who was actually kind of attractive, but she made fun of him, jabbing verbally at him in front of their friends. In fact, she went so far as to complain publicly to others about his sexual failures; he was "not a man in bed," she would sneer, with him standing two feet away.

All of these putdowns, these inadequacies, built up, one on top of another. Lee didn't talk about it, but basically just suffered in silence. After his wife dumped him and moved in with

88

a friend, he would sit alone in front of an old black-and-white TV set and watch thrillers and murder mysteries. His eyes looked kind of glassed over, but deep inside the volcano of resentment was quietly boiling. "He was slowly going mad," Manchester wrote later.

And finally, on a Friday morning, when he rode to work with a friend of his, as things turned out, that package of curtain rods in the back seat wasn't really curtain rods after all. And Lee, pouring all of his resentment into one act of violent payback, pulled the trigger of his mail-order Mannlicher-Carcano, and sent bullets crashing into President John F. Kennedy.

That's how deadly resentment can be if we let it build up. That's the end result of rage that isn't resolved. And yes, it's what can happen if we memorize and keep singing the theme song: "I Can't Stop HATING You!"

In his book, *The Death of a President,* William Manchester points out how in a very impersonal, long-distance way, Lee Harvey Oswald resented everything Kennedy had that he didn't have. Kennedy was rich and tanned and powerful, and Lee had none of those privileges. And day by day, as his life aimlessly and bitterly tumbled toward November 22, 1963, he simply couldn't get past his resentments. He couldn't turn his mind in any other direction.

Think a bit more just now about the other person in our rage relationship, the person we hate. If I can borrow some more music, this time from Linda Ronstadt, I recall those complaining lyrics: "I been cheated, been mistreated. When will I be loved?" And maybe it's no accident that it's also a Ronstadt hit which goes this way: "You're no good, you're no good, you're no good . . . baby, you're no good." Because most of the time, our resentments in life are aimed at that other person. We can't be happy unless they're no good AND unless the entire rest of the world agrees with us that they're no good. We'd like to stand up in church and point at them and cry out: "Can I get a witness? They're no good!"

Going back to the "blind" motif of the previous chapter, there's another tragic bit of truth in life that we often don't realize, but the Lee Harvey Oswald story painfully points it out. A good deal of the time, we are resenting a person, or their behavior, and frankly, the person we're obsessing about has absolutely no idea that we're angry. They're a thousand miles away and completely clueless.

Think about it. Did President Kennedy in the White House know that a sulking former Marine, estranged from his smart-mouthed Russian wife, was huddled in loneliness there in a small Fort Worth house? Did he know anything about the poisonous thoughts Lee was thinking as JFK and his younger brother Bobby weathered the Cuban missile crisis and then planned the trip to Dallas? Of course not. And yet Lee Harvey Oswald spent literally hours each day resenting, fondling his hatreds, plotting ways to get even with the world, hatching schemes to make those rich, tuxedoed Kennedys pay a price for their undeserved good fortunes.

Remember again that Roger Ebert line about grudges: "Someone should tell them that resentment is just a way of letting someone else use your mind rent-free." And this is true both in our personal relationships and also in the spiritual realm. Why should that enemy be permitted to use your mind that way, to torture you with thoughts of hate, and not pay any rent? He doesn't even know you're spending all that energy on him! What a deadly trap it is!

And even more sobering a realization is how the enemy of this world, Satan, does the same thing. Resentment is his choicest tool! Imagine the price tag he puts on it. If we could put a price tag on the hours and days—maybe even adding up to years—where we've mulled over how angry we are with someone, we can't imagine the celebrating he does. And of course, those hours come right out of the time we could be reading God's Word, praying, sharing Christ with others, forgetting ourselves as we serve others.

There's a tragic story in the Old Testament book of 1 Kings, chapter 12, where a new king, Rehoboam, had just inherited the throne from his father, Solomon. And all the people, resentful over years of heavy oppression and taxation, sent a delegation to the king asking for some relief. They'd harbored anger for years and now they were finally communicating. Things had boiled over.

And as you read the story, it's clear that this king was completely out of touch. Clueless! He couldn't even relate to their resentment. He asked two groups of advisors, "How shall I respond? Shall I ease up?" One group said Yes, but the other bunch, a collection of real tough Generation Xers said, "No, man, pile it on. Let them know who's boss. Tell them we're tripling the size of the IRS; we're moving from whips to scorpions." And this aloof king, Rehoboam, so out of touch with the resentment of the people, went with the advice from the under-30 set. And as a result, the kingdom split in two and was never reunited again.

What do we do, then, with our rage? W. R. Alger once wrote—and we don't want this: "Men often make up in wrath what they want in reason."

And we remember the twin bits of advice coming to us from across the years. First, the ancient Chinese proverb: "Never answer a letter (or respond to email!) when you are angry."

Then Mark Twain's rather unscriptural advice from *Pudd'nhead Wilson*: "When angry, count four; when very angry, swear."

Certainly I don't advise you to do that in communicating about your resentment! But what do we do?

We probably would do better to take counsel from our Bibles instead of Samuel Clemens this time. Mark down these two classic gems from the book of Proverbs: "He that is slow to anger is better than the mighty; and he that ruleth his spirit than he that taketh a city." (16:32, KJV)

We should extrapolate here and suggest that the person who's slow and cautious in *expressing* his anger is equally wise. Sometimes resentments do need to be verbalized, especially if we want to lay aside our burden of anger before sundown as the Bible teaches. But let's be slow to anger and slow to express anger. Let's pray over each word before we say it; let's get down on our knees before we compose that email attack memo and get down on our knees a second time before we hit the SEND button.

And then, just one chapter earlier, Proverbs 15:1, we read these great words: "A gentle answer turns away wrath, but a harsh word stirs up anger."

How many people have brought a feud to an end with that gentle, soft answer? It's been suggested that these five words—"I was wrong. I'm sorry"—are among the most powerful on this planet. In his classic bestseller, *How to Win Friends and Influence People,* Dale Carnegie advises people to say this to an adversary: "I may be wrong. I frequently am. Let's examine the facts."

Right here we should cross over to the other side of the field and think for a moment about what's happening there. Resentment is bad, but being a person who needlessly *causes* resentment—well, that's even worse. Why should the people of God live in such a way as to consistently create such bitterness and simmering rage? Why should we who are bosses and leaders and spouses conduct our affairs with such insensitivity that those beneath us are resentful and angry?

Always Mad at Mr. Oblivious

It's ironic to note that these two marvelous Bible gems about being slow to anger and using the soft reply were written by King Solomon! Here's the king whose insensitivity and heavy taxation helped lead to the kingdom split of his son Rehoboam! His words were good, but what a greater blessing he could have been if he had lived as a true and humble God-fearing monarch.

And for you and me today, how about some soft words from us? On both ends of this equation we call resentment? Can we live, on the one side, forgiving lives? And on the other side, attractive lives that don't need too much forgiveness? It'd be nice to get our favorite country-western song back the way we like it: "I Can't Stop LOVING You!"

13

Giving Your Grudges to the President

You see an actor on TV screaming into a telephone: "I'm so mad, I'd like that guy's teeth kicked in!" And you wonder: "'Wow—who in the world is he talking to like that?" Would it surprise you to find that people in the Bible got on the hotline and shouted at God using exactly those words?

Back in October 2000, right before the famous "dimpled chad" election and the Florida marathon, *Newsweek* pointed to some of the hard issues America's new Commander in Chief— Gore or Bush—would have to deal with in the many ragged regions of the world. Ehud Barak versus Yasir Arafat. The suicide attack on the *U.S.S. Cole* in Yemen. What would Putin do next in Russia? Could Kostunica manage things in Serbia and keep Milosevic out of the way as he tried to bring his people into a new era of freedom? And *Newsweek* lamented with this troubling line for the new president to consider: "America is now Goliath, facing many Davids—enemies who use stealth, speed and suicide to draw blood. What can we do?"

And those of us with American passports, whether we travel to the world's hot spots, or just get in line for the Matterhorn ride at Disneyland, have to ponder this question: Is the president up to all this? All of this gets taken to him and dumped on his desk. "Here, Mr. President. Make this go away." Is he tough enough? Can the buck really and truly stop there, or should the American people hold back a few nickels and dimes?

Have you ever longed to just unleash a venom-laced diatribe of hatred against someone who has hurt you? In your mind, you've practiced and fine-tuned that speech until it glowed with purple passion and power. Oh, it was good! It rhymed like a Jesse Jackson sermon. It cut up your enemy until there weren't any two square inches left of him.

In Yancey's book, *The Bible Jesus Read,* there's an entire chapter on some of the screaming fits you can actually find in the book of Psalms. Almost on every page King David is throwing verbal javelins at his enemies—or actually, asking God to do the honors. Here's just a random slice from Psalm 68: "May God arise, may his enemies be scattered; may his foes flee before him. As smoke is blown away by the wind, may you blow them away; as wax melts before the fire, may the wicked perish before God" (vs. 1, 2).

Back in chapter 58, he gets even more graphic: "Break the teeth in their mouths, O God." He's speaking of the wicked here. "Tear out, O Lord, the fangs of the lions!" (v. 6). Then down just four verses he adds: "The righteous will be glad when they are avenged, when they bathe their feet in the blood of the wicked."

What's the point of all this violent, teeth-knocking-out Scripture? Yancey actually lifts up King David's mad-as-a-wet-hen prayers as being the right way to approach the issue of our own unresolved anger. "If a person wrongs me unjustly," he writes, "I have several options. I can seek personal revenge, a response condemned by the Bible. I can deny or suppress my feelings of anger and hurt. Or I can take those feelings to God, entrusting God with the task of 'retributive justice.' "

Then Yancey adds this: "The cursing psalms are vivid examples of that last option. 'It is Mine to avenge; I will repay,' says the Lord—prayers like the cursing psalms place vengeance in the proper hands. Significantly, the cursing psalms express their outrage to God, not to the enemy."

That's a marvelous insight, isn't it? When you're boiling mad inside, when you're burning with resentment, sometimes those feelings are not wrong. But where should they go? The Bible tells us that Option One is not appropriate: getting revenge yourself. Proverbs 20:22 says: "Do not say, 'I'll pay you back for this wrong!' Wait for the Lord, and he will deliver you."

Suppressing and stifling our anger is also wrong; the Bible tells us not to let our grudges continue past sundown. But here Option Three is clearly and plainly endorsed. We can take our frustrations, our pent-up anger, our grudges, march right into the White House of the universe, go straight into the Oval Office, and say to the President—actually to the Lord God Almighty, Jehovah: "Here. You want it—You got it." That's exactly what the Bible tells us to do. Go boldly into the throne room of grace, and give that rotten, anger-causing scenario to God. Because the buck stops there, and so does the bellyaching.

Yancey goes on to observe in amazement that our screams, our howls of rage, are apparently not threatening to God at all, not off-putting. He doesn't mind! "Instinctively, we want to 'clean up' our feelings in our prayers, but perhaps we have it all backwards. Perhaps we should strive to take all our worst feelings to God. After all, what would be gossip when addressed to anyone else is petition when addressed to God. What is a vengeful curse when spoken about someone ('Damn those people!') is a plea of helpless dependence when spoken directly to God ('It's up to You to damn those people, since You only are a just Judge.')"

My instinct would be to apologize for those "D" words, or to blame Philip Yancey and say, "Hey, I'm only passing along his spicy language." But how often have we thought the "D" word about someone? And isn't it precisely the job of God the righteous Judge to decide if a person is to be damned, or lost? Take your angry thoughts on that matter and put them on His desk. He doesn't mind. He doesn't call Security or the Secret Service and have you thrown out into the Rose Garden.

Yancey follows up with a personal confession: "I have made it a weekly practice, on a long walk on the hill behind my home, to present to God my anger against people who have wronged me. I recount all my reasons for feeling unfairly treated or misunderstood, forcing myself to open up deep feelings to God (does God not know them anyway?)" Then he confesses this: "I can testify that the outpouring itself has a therapeutic effect. Usually I come away feeling as if I have just released a huge burden. The unfairness no longer sticks like a thorn inside me, as it once did; I have expressed it aloud to someone—to God."

It's hard to imagine being there in the Oval Office, and having the president listen patiently as we ventilate. And then he calmly hits a buzzer and an aide comes in. "Steve, take care of my friend here," he says. "Whatever he needs." Or he picks up a telephone, calls an important Army leader and directs him to unleash all of the nation's military hardware, its juggernaut of power, to solve my problem. He's not flummoxed by my dilemma; he's not confused or in a quandary. He simply calls upon all his resources, and takes care of my need.

And our unflappable Leader is interested in our needs—both large and small. The late, great Erma Bombeck once articulated

97

the deepest spiritual cry of many, many people. Here was her daily prayer: "Lord, if You can't make me thin, then make my friends look fat."

Can you relate to that? The Bible is filled with similar prayers. "Make my enemies look fat." "Make them lose all their money." "Lord, if it's not too much bother, would You please just up and kill them all? You can do it, Lord! If You'll just smite all my enemies dead, I won't ask You for another thing the rest of this month."

It's interesting that the Bible writers went through a kind of spiritual schizophrenia. Just a few pages over from where the psalmist cries to heaven for revenge, the son of the psalmist, Solomon, writes this in chapter 24 of Proverbs: "Do not gloat when your enemy falls; when he stumbles, do not let your heart rejoice, or the Lord will see and disapprove and turn his wrath away from him" (vs. 17, 18).

That's an odd suggestion, isn't it? If we act too happy about our enemy getting whacked, God might stop whacking him just to teach us a lesson. Should we pretend we're not partying over our antagonist's demise, or only celebrate in the closet where God can't see us?

In *What's So Amazing About Grace?* Philip Yancey retells the devastating story out of Simon Wiesenthal's book, *The Sunflower*. Back in 1944, World War II, Wiesenthal saw the worst of Nazism. He was a POW in Poland, and saw Hitler's brigades kill his grandmother. They kidnapped his mother, stuffed her into a cattle-car train headed for the camps. All told, he lost something like eighty-nine of his relatives to the Holocaust. He himself tried unsuccessfully to commit suicide when first taken prisoner.

And there's one story, one anecdote, where he's at a German hospital, forced to help clean up. And he's summoned to the bedside of a dying Nazi, a man wrapped from head to toe with bandages. He wants to confess to a Jew, any Jew, his sins. And in a raspy voice this Karl admits how he and his fellow Nazis, in the town of Dnyepropetrovsk, rounded up 300-plus Jews and herded them into a three-story building. Dousing it with gas, they then lit this human bonfire, shooting anybody who tried to get out of the burning building. It was a horrible, evil scene, and now this Nazi soldier was trying to confess. "In the last hours of my life you are with me," he croaked. "I do not know who you are, I know only that you are a Jew and that is enough."

And he wanted Simon Wiesenthal to give him absolution, to forgive him. Just those four words, "Yes, I forgive you," would have sent Karl to a peaceful death. And Wiesenthal, standing there in his prison garb, with the yellow Star of David on his shabby uniform, couldn't say the words. He *wouldn't* say them. Without uttering a syllable, he turned around and walked out of the room. This man's crimes, the evil of the Third Reich, the burning of those 300 Jews, the slaughter of his own grandmother—it was all too much to forgive. There was just no way.

More than twenty years later, Simon Wiesenthal wrote to many theologians and priests and rabbis, asking them about this agonizing memory of his. "What should I have done?" he asked. "Should I have forgiven this German criminal for his sins?" He got thirty-two answers from these religious people. Only six suggested that maybe he should have offered forgiveness. Others pointed out that morally, Wiesenthal could only forgive sins done to *him*. One quoted the ancient poet, Dryden: "Forgiveness, *to the injured,* doth belong."

And then Yancey sums up with this: "A few of the Jewish respondents said that the enormity of Nazi crimes had exceeded all possibility of forgiveness. Herbert Gold, an American author and professor, declared, 'The guilt for this horror lies so heavily on the Germans of that time that no personal reaction to it is unjustifiable.' Said another, 'The millions of innocent people who were tortured and slaughtered would have to come back to life before I could forgive.' Novelist Cynthia Ozick was fierce: 'Let the SS man die unshriven [meaning without absolution]. Let him go to hell.' A Christian writer confessed, 'I think I would strangle him in his bed.' "

Well, this story may seem far beyond the boundary of what the human race can ever cope with. Except that these people did cope with it. This is what happened to them. And I relate it here for two reasons. First of all, perhaps it brings into perspective our trivial hurts, the smallness of our ongoing feud with that certain someone. Is our anger really justified? Are we perhaps playing with our petty resentment TOO much?

But here's the more important issue. Is it possible that some things absolutely *cannot* be forgiven? Is the Holocaust so big, so horrendous, so beyond the pale, that it simply drains away all of heaven's storehouses of grace . . . and still is found wanting? I asked once in a Christmas radio program if perhaps Oklahoma bomber Timothy McVeigh simply could not be redeemed, even by heaven. Maybe Calvary itself, that monumental sacrifice for the human race, isn't enough to wash away the wrongful deaths of 168 innocent victims. Is it possible that even the president cannot pardon *this?*

Well, in our humanity, perhaps it's understandable that we might think so. And I confess here that I don't know your hurt. I don't know who has wounded you, and to what extent. All I do know is what the Bible says. And when John the Baptist looks up and sees Jesus coming toward him, he says without any doubt: "Look, the Lamb of God, who takes away the sin of the WORLD!"

Giving Your Grudges to the President

How to stack up the Friday afternoon of Calvary against the universal blot of sin we call the Holocaust? The burning of those 300 Jews? The slaughter of Oklahoma City's 168 men and women and teenagers and children and babies? You saw that picture too, where the fireman brings out that dead baby. Isn't that so big, so monstrous, that even God Himself will not or perhaps even cannot forgive it?

I would think that, and you would think that. But the plain Word of God tells us that Jesus Christ is able to take away all sin, wash away all evil. All sins can be forgiven unless the sinner resolutely turns away and rejects the Holy Spirit's attempts.

What that means is this. Every time a person clings to hatred, or holds on to his anger, he is in essence saying this: Calvary is not enough for this one. Heaven is not big enough. God is not good enough, powerful enough. The blood of my Savior is not potent enough to cover this wrong . . . and that's why I have to continually and eternally keep stoking this fire myself. If vengeance is needed, I can't trust that God will handle it; I need to stay on *this* job myself.

If we make a spiritual statement that forgiveness is simply giving a person up to God, surrendering that person and their deeds and your resentments and bitterness to a strong Savior, then what is tested is your daily and hourly *belief* in that Savior, in the strength of that God. Forgiveness really tests your Christian faith, your connection with God. Is our God "able," as the songs all say? Can we trust Him to handle the tyranny of our enemy, to pay back the evil we're surrendering to Him?

It's very interesting that in Luke 17, where Jesus talks about forgiving other people, He spells out that if someone sins against you even seven times in a day, you're obligated to forgive him. So Jesus knew that we would often experience the simmering rage of repetitive wrongdoing, of daily insensitivity. Christ knew that there would come situations where that certain person would get to us, not with one horrible act of violence or murder, but just all the time! And His instructions are clear: forgive him. Forgive him seven times a day if you have to.

But it's the next sentence that's so interesting. In verse five, the apostles all said with one voice: "Lord, increase our faith!"

And maybe we say, "Huh? What does faith have to do with forgiving?" And the answer is plain. Unless we have faith in a mighty God, unless we've put our lives and our destinies and our need for revenge in *His* hands, we're simply incapable of letting go of that wicked person. We can't do it.

Maybe you don't think it out as articulately as that. Most likely, if you're like the rest of us, you just hang on to anger because it's enjoyable to do so, to love hatred. And we don't easily give up the things we love. But it's the long testimony of the human experience that this hatred we love turns around and destroys us in the end.

Yancey shares a final comment: "Not to forgive imprisons me in the past and locks out all potential for change. I thus yield control to another, my enemy, and doom myself to suffer the consequences of the wrong. I once heard an immigrant rabbi make an astonishing statement. 'Before coming to America, I had to forgive Adolf Hitler,' he said. 'I did not want to bring Hitler inside me to my new country.' "

Do you have an Adolf Hitler to leave behind before you enter a new country? Believe me, God is big enough.

One more point about shouting and screaming in His presence. Going back a president or so to a guy from Arkansas named Bill, I have two books, one by Bob Woodward, the other by George Stephanopoulos, and they both describe the temper of the former president. Stephanopoulos, often on the receiving end, called Clinton's tantrums "purple fits" or "earthquakes."

Giving Your Grudges to the President

Or sometimes just "the wave." When the president got mad enough, he could go one-on-one with King David for sure. "I want him dead, dead!" he screamed about one incompetent aide. "I want him horse-whipped."

And when we get down on our knees for an "imprecatory prayer session" with God ourselves, we think, "Maybe I shouldn't do that. Maybe I should tone it down, 'watch my language.' " Yancey weighs in on that question too: "As the books of Job, Jeremiah, and Habakkuk clearly show, God has a high threshold of tolerance for what is appropriate to say in a prayer." After all, a "jeremiad" is essentially just that: a screaming tantrum. "God can 'handle,' " Yancey writes, "my unsuppressed rage. I may well find that my vindictive feelings need God's correction—but only by taking those feelings to God will I have that opportunity for correction and healing."

Well, that's where we are. We've got a President to take our frustrations to, a Leader with plenty of experience. Especially at listening.

14

Forgiveness
Times Seven

Jasper, Texas. Laramie, Wyoming. These are names that remind us of cruelty, of pent-up anger . . . and now of simmering grudges that won't go away anytime soon. Can those crimes be forgiven? Buried in the police books is an older case that was seven times worse.

Is there something *right now* that you're having a hard time forgiving? That's OK; we all sometimes have to struggle with the temptation to play with and caress a certain mental "list."

I'd like to give you both the long form and the short form of what Vera Sinton suggests are some of the main things a victim might legitimately have a grudge about. Here's her list of seven hard, hard things that would be agony to forgive . . . and attached are one or two "snapshot" illustrations of each.

1. *An injustice carried out for cynical political ends.* My first reaction goes back more than a decade to poor Michael Dukakis, whose presidential campaign was upended by the famous Willie Horton ad. On his deathbed, political operative Lee Atwater confessed to some regret for the unfairness of that racist attack ad.

Historians will remember that a certain Alexander Hamilton didn't just get his feelings hurt over a political discussion. Vice President Aaron Burr actually shot and killed Hamilton in a duel, clear back in 1804. Compared to Mr. Hamilton, I'd say Dukakis got off rather lightly.

Here's #2: *The jealous destruction of a man because of his good influence over others.* A name like Martin Luther King, Jr., or Mohandas Gandhi, immediately comes to mind.

How about this one? #3: *Being betrayed for money by someone you trusted.* You'll understand that a Christian preacher goes right away to that great old Bible story about Joseph, who was sold by his brothers. And maybe, in the realm of fiction and Hollywood, we'd think of, perhaps, Michael Corleone, whose trusted lieutenant, the *caporegime*—Tessio—betrayed his boss to the Barzini family. That's not such a good example, because everyone in that story was backstabbing everyone else; the Godfather's laundry was dirtier than anybody's. But the illustration of selling out for cash is still there.

Here's a hard one: Vera's #4 reason. *Desertion by a close companion at the moment of danger, denying all knowledge of you.* Maybe you've read the marvelous book from World War II, one of my favorites, entitled *Flee the Captor,* where a young Christian named John Weidner helped more than a thousand refugees escape from the Nazis. But there's a story in that book about a man named Joseph Smit, who liquidated his family's entire fortune and gave it to one of these "passers," a man skilled in the so-called underground routes out of Germany and occupied France. Things were going just great until right at the crucial juncture, with the most difficult barbed-wire checkpoints just ahead and Gestapo gendarmes everywhere. All of a sudden, this "passer" was gone. Checked out . . . and with all of Joseph Smit's money with him.

Fortunately, Weidner, as a dedicated Christian, stepped in and arranged—using his own funds and risking his own life—to help the family get across the border to Switzerland. But imagine that empty feeling, helpless anger: no money, no food, no friends—and the person who had promised to stay with you and help you: GONE.

Here's #5 in Vera Sinton's list, and remember that her book has this title: *How Can I Forgive?* Can you relate to this one? *Beating someone up for a bit of fun.* And here in America, we think in shame about men like James Byrd, Jr., and Matthew Shepard, who were both tortured and killed because they were different. Imagine the struggles the parents and relatives are having even now, trying to resolve their anger, trying to give God the deep hurt in their hearts.

#6: *Allowing an innocent man to be sentenced to death.* Also here in the U.S. we've had a rash of death-row reversals recently and police scandals, as it's discovered that witnesses have lied and law enforcement officials have manufactured evidence. In Illinois, they suspended the death sentence after finding out that they had had twelve executions, and thirteen capital convictions overturned. "We aren't even batting .500," said Governor George Ryan in announcing the moratorium. But imagine the anger if someone were to knowingly and deliberately and willfully allow a wrong conviction to stand—and it was your son they strapped down to a lethal injection gurney.

Now the final point on Vera's checklist. #7: *Standing and jeering at a person in excruciating pain.* And going back to #5, we could put on the top of this "Wanted" poster Russell Henderson and Aaron McKinley from the Laramie hanging, and then the trio of thugs from Jasper, Texas—Lawrence Brewer, John William King, and Shawn Allen Berry—who dragged a man behind a pickup truck and laughed as they watched him die. And of course, down through the sad pages of human history, we have men like the infamous Josef Mengele, the doctor whose horrific deeds are chronicled in *The Rise and Fall of the Third Reich.* Mengele devised "experiments," which he did on Jewish prisoners, watching impassively, taking notes, as men and women were subjected to the cruelest kinds of torture: measuring how fast a man will freeze to death, for instance.

And again we ask, as we think about this list: how could you forgive if you, or someone you loved, had endured even one of these seven unbelievable atrocities? How could you give such a thing to God? How could the words, "Father, forgive them," possibly have any meaning?

Well, we can go right down that whole list of seven outrages, seven forgiveness-blockers, and notice that it's Jesus, more than anyone, who endured, not one, but all seven of these hurts.

Here's Sinton's list of shame again. #1: *Injustice carried out for cynical political ends.* That's Jesus, certainly. #2: *The jealous destruction of a man because of his good influence over others.* That's precisely why the Pharisees and Sadducees were so angry with Jesus. #3: *Being betrayed for money by someone you trusted.* Do the initials J.I.—for Judas Iscariot—ring any bells? #4: *Desertion by a close companion at the moment of danger, denying all knowledge of you.* And of course, what Peter did to Jesus, three times before the rooster crowed almost defines the word "denial," doesn't it?

#5: *Beating someone up for a bit of fun.* Here's the court transcript from Luke 22:63, 64, according to *The Message* paraphrase: "The men in charge of Jesus began poking fun at Him, slapping Him around. They put a blindfold on Him and taunted, 'Who hit you that time?' They were having a grand time with Him."

Does that sound like shades of Jasper, Texas?

On to #6: *Allowing an innocent man to be sentenced to one of the cruelest deaths ever devised.* That's precisely what Pontius Pilate did, washing his hands in that basin, saying, "Don't blame me." And yet he had to sign off on the D.O.E.—the "Date of Execution" official order.

And finally, #7: *Standing and jeering at a person in excruciating pain.* Around the cross on that Friday afternoon, the vendors sold soda and Cracker Jack as the crowds hooted at Jesus up on the cross. Luke 23:35-37: "The people stood there staring at Jesus, and the ringleaders made faces, taunting. 'He saved others. Let's see Him save Himself! The Messiah of God—ha! The Chosen—ha!' The soldiers also came up and poked fun at Him, making a game of it. They toasted Him with sour wine: 'So You're King of the Jews! Save Yourself!' " " 'If You're a king, where's Your army? Aren't they going to come and rescue You?' "

Listen, you and I can't ever say, "My load is too big to ever forgive! It's beyond grace, beyond forgiving. It's too much." Jesus went through this ordeal, this marathon of seven soul-shredding attacks, every single one of them unjustified. And yet He forgave the people involved . . . right at that very moment! While the nails were going in! While the spit was hitting His face. While the taunts were ringing in His ears.

Vera Sinton concludes this list of seven and writes: "Jesus, God's Son, is the only sinless person who has ever lived. While all these things were happening to Jesus, He was loving the people involved, offering friendship to the one who betrayed Him, warning His companions of danger ahead. He gently challenged the governor who sentenced Him. He openly prayed for the soldiers who nailed His hands and feet to a cross."

108

And how? How did Jesus live up to His own words about forgiving seven times, and even seventy times seven? How did He not only not nurse a grudge, He didn't even let one begin? He was forgiving as the sins happened.

Well, we're in Luke 23. If the challenge is there, maybe the answer is too. And sure enough, you just go down nine verses, and there it is. Verse 46: "Jesus called loudly, 'Father, I place My life in Your hands!' "

Whether you're the relatives of Matthew Shepard, or Coretta Scott King, or just someone whose co-workers have ripped you off at the office, those eight words can really spell the end of our inner torment. "Father, I place my life in Your hands." "Father, I give it all . . . to You."

15

Long-distance
Death on Omaha Beach

*"I didn't hate Jews," he said in his last confessions. And this was
Albert Speer, Hitler's minister of armaments. That's a remarkable
statement from a Nazi killer: "I didn't hate Jews." But then the P.S.
"I was indifferent to them." And that indifference, that distance,
made Speer a Holocaust butcher.*

There was an exceptional article that appeared in the official
weekly magazine for my denomination, the *Adventist Review*.
And the title by Miroslav M. Kis is this: "Who Is My Enemy?"
That's a twist, of course, on the parable where a man asked Jesus:
"Who is my neighbor?"

Professor Kis, who teaches theology and ethics at Andrews
University in Michigan, comes from an Eastern European
background in the Ukraine, and he leads into his article by
 describing how his family used to live in Croatia, Serbia, and
Bosnia. And he didn't find any huge differences—comparing
the twenty-five years he lived there to the thirty years of peace
and prosperity he's enjoyed in the West. In fact, he writes:
"All we remember are the different cultural expressions of
kindness."

In other words, people are people. There's good everywhere and bad everywhere. Bombs and bouquets in all countries. But he goes on to describe what makes an enemy, what makes a grudge. The kicker to his article is this line: "Dismantling the walls that divide us." Well, what ingredient most builds up that wall? And his answer is one word long: distance. "Distance is of the essence in creating and maintaining animosity," he writes. "It is nearly impossible to kill someone at 'close range.' Closeness is almost always an antidote to enmity."

Perhaps you saw the wrenching war film, *Saving Private Ryan,* directed by Steven Spielberg. Talk about a portrayal of enmity, of bloodshed! Those first twenty-five minutes are probably the most brutally accurate cinematic picture of the horror of war ever filmed. But most of the time, it was bloodshed from a distance: a machine gun raking the sand and the water at Omaha Beach, Normandy, June 6, 1944. You looked through your gunsights and saw a distant figure, and you squeezed the trigger, and that figure toppled over in the red-soaked water. A character named Daniel Boone Jackson was a sharpshooter GI from Hickory Valley, Tennessee. Ironically, he would quietly whisper a prayer—"Blessed be the Lord my strength, which teacheth my hands to war, and my fingers to fight," quoting from Psalm 144—as he picked off one German soldier after another. There in the final battle scenes, this American sniper was up in a church bell tower, praying and firing away until a Tiger tank got him. But it was long-distance death, anonymous warfare.

Far more horrifying was a mercifully brief scene where a German and an American were locked in mortal combat in the upstairs of the bombed-out building at Ramelle. Now the distance was gone. They were eyeball to eyeball, gouging, tearing at each other. Then finally, slowly, the German leaned into his enemy with a knife, snuffing out a farmboy's life from just six inches away. And that was the worst, because that kind of closeness is in stark, horrible contrast to the distance one usually needs in order to hate and fight and maim and kill.

In this magazine article by Dr. Kis, he tells us that the Bible word, *oyebh,* in Hebrew, doesn't just refer to an enemy, but specifically means an enemy or assailant who "comes from outside to inflict personal or national injury." Someone who comes in from "out there," from a distance, to hurt you.

And in our own personal relationships, even if you and I live a long way from Bosnia, it's this same problem: distance is what fuels our grudges. We allow our anger to put many miles, at least emotional ones, between us and that person we're angry with. Where once we saw eye to eye, and felt close to each other, and talked and openly shared, a drifting away happens . . . and soon it's easy to hate them. Dr. Kis tells us—and remember, he teaches both religion and ethics, so this is a field of up-close study for him—that the first stage in "enemy-making" is this: identity. "Our search for identity often moves in a negative direction. Our self-affirmation comes at the expense of another."

This negative quest for identity, he writes, takes us down four bad roads: "The distance of difference," "The distance of derision," "The distance of defamation," and "The distance of indifference." First I notice the things that are different; maybe I slip into a pattern of telling ethnic jokes. Then I begin to ridicule this person I used to have as a friend. Then it goes to defamation, open name-calling. And finally, the distance of indifference. I stop caring at all.

Kis reminds us that the first grudge in the Bible ends up with God asking Cain: "Hey, where's your brother? Your *brother!*" And Cain shrugs. "How should I know? Am I his keeper? Leave me alone!" Speaking of *Saving Private Ryan* and World War II, Kis quotes from Albert Speer, who served as Adolf Hitler's minister of armaments. "If I had continued to see them as human beings," Speer confesses, "I would not have remained a Nazi. I did not hate them. I was indifferent to them."

That made it possible for the Nazis at Auschwitz to bargain with a nearby chemical company, I. G. Farben, which wanted 150 women to use in an experiment. They wouldn't pay more than 170 marks a head. Notice: not a "person," just "a head." A few weeks later, another memo was sent. "The tests were made. All subjects died. We shall contact you shortly on the subject of a new load."

Chilling, isn't it? And it begins with distance. These weren't women, or even prisoners. Just scribbles on a sheet of paper. 170 marks a head. The "subjects." We need "a new load." When you permit yourself to bear a grudge, to allow distance to form between you and an enemy, this is the direction you head in. You begin to steer your tank toward Auschwitz and the ovens.

I'll be the first to confess that "distance" and enmity are rather comfortable things for us. It's easy to push someone away because you hate them, and then hate them because they are far away. It's hard to go to someone, when you'd just as soon have a few oceans separating you, and say: "Look, enough is enough. I was wrong. I don't want to hate you or have you hate me. I don't want to be an *oyebh,* an outside enemy, or keep thinking of you as one. Can we get close? Or at least take a step toward each other, try to understand each other?"

Back in the first century A.D., of course, there was a certain amount of enmity between Jews and non-Jews. "Distance" was their favorite word back then, just as we continue to embrace it now, not only in the Middle East but in our own neighborhoods. In *The Message,* Dr. Eugene Peterson's paraphrase of Ephesians 2:13, 14 explicitly mentions this very idea of distance: "The Messiah has made things up between us so that we're now together on this"—God's great salvation plan—"both non-Jewish outsiders and Jewish insiders. He tore down the wall we used to keep each other at a distance. He repealed the law code that had become so clogged with fine print and footnotes that it hindered more than it helped. Then He started over. Instead of continuing with two groups separated by centuries of animosity and suspicion, He created a new kind of human being, a fresh start for everybody."

Notice: "The wall we used to keep each other *at a distance.*" Here's a bit more: "Christ brought us together through His death on the Cross. The Cross got us to embrace, and that was the end of the hostility. Christ came and preached peace to you outsiders and peace to us insiders. He treated us as equals, and so made us equals. Through Him we both share the same Spirit and have equal access to the Father."

That's some mind-boggling theology, to be sure. But think about that person you hate so much, and about the Grand Canyon grudge that's standing in the way. Is that person saved by the Cross—just like you? Yes. Does that person have access to the Holy Spirit—just like you? Yes. Equal access to the Father— just like you? Yes. Does the Father love him as He loves you? Did Jesus die equally for him as for you; shed His blood for the both of you, despite this current barrier? And of course, that family genealogy chart in your old King James Bible tells you clearly that any two people having the same Dad . . . are brothers. Or brother and sister.

So Paul writes: "Christ brought us together through His death on the Cross. The Cross got us to embrace" . . . at least, it's supposed to get us to embrace. It sounds brutal to say, and I look with shame into my own heart, but there should be no grudges—none, not a one, zero—among the people of God. To have a grudge is to deny the power of the Cross. It's as plain as that. May God have mercy on us all, as we aim away from Auschwitz and toward Calvary.

CHAPTER 16

Gaining Strength From the Storm

Would God ever let you have an enemy for a purpose? A small hurt now, to get you ready for an earthquake hurt a year from now? Instead of screaming at the sky, "God, please take this horrible person out of my life!" perhaps we should ask instead: "Lord, what are You trying to teach me?"

People called him "the boy bishop" when he received that high title at the very young age of thirty-eight. Later, at sixty-eight, he was to receive the informal name, "America's senior cardinal." Joseph Bernardin was the much-beloved archbishop of Chicago and there were a lot of Catholics who thought that he might well become the first American pope someday.

I have a marvelous book written by a friend of the cardinal, Eugene Kennedy. The two men took such different paths: Bernardin moving up through the ranks, adding more and more influence to his résumé, while Kennedy, once a fellow priest, eventually left the priesthood in order to marry. And Kennedy, in this moving biography, entitled *My Brother Joseph*, speaks in awe of the quiet strength Bernardin possessed. "I would learn at close range [over 30 years], when nobody else was looking, how profoundly manly he was," Kennedy writes, "in a gentle, non-argumentative style that covered the tensile strength of his character."

Kennedy found out firsthand about that "tensile strength"—meaning strength that can meet stress and tension, strength that can bend but not break. When he wanted to leave the Catholic priesthood to marry his "Sally," Dr. Sara Charles, the woman he had fallen in love with, he needed Joseph Bernardin to help with the formal church process of laicization, the petitions needed to leave his priesthood vows. And Joseph kindly said that he would help within the limits of his office. But it would be complicated; it could take a long time, and there were certainly political issues involved.

Then Kennedy kind of leaned into him with a hard, hard request. "You could marry us," he said—a request that would be plainly outside the bounds of church law. And Kennedy writes: "I had forced him into harm's way in that place where real friendship collided with sworn duty."

After just a moment, this quiet strong man shook his head. "I can't do that. Even if I wanted to, I can't do that." And he explained that he had a higher loyalty, to his church and to its teachings.

Well, even as a Protestant Christian, I salute people who are faithful to what they feel are the doctrines and creeds of their chosen church family. But there's another lesson to be learned from the life of this remarkable servant of God. First, he en-dured a public scandal when people accused him of helping to overthrow his predecessor, Cardinal Cody. Then the bigger bombshell: on November 12, 1993, in U.S. District Court, Southern District of Ohio, Western Division, Case #0-1-93-0784 was filed on behalf of a plaintiff named Steven Cook, who alleged that

Cardinal Joseph Bernardin had sexually abused him while Steven was a minor.

You might recall the story because it kind of rocked the nation for a while. The archbishop of Chicago? Molesting a young troubled man, just a teenager?

But Cardinal Bernardin responded with honest, forthright Christian love. He prayed his way through the crisis. He patiently answered insulting questions from reporters. He actually sat down and wrote a personal letter to the very man who was accusing him: Steven Cook. "You must be suffering a great deal. The idea came to me yesterday morning that it would be a good thing if I visited with you personally. The purpose of the visit would be strictly pastoral—to show my concern for you and to pray with you."

The media circus lasted more than three months—108 days to be exact—before Steven Cook recanted the charges he had made in court. None of it had been true, and Bernardin stepped in front of the microphones in Chicago and said to the reporters: "*Deo gratias*—thanks be to God."

Think about what an opportunity this could have been for one of the major grudges of all time to be birthed. A false accusation. Public scrutiny: Kennedy later told his friend Joseph that he was very likely "the most investigated man in America, and the man with the cleanest slate—nobody had been able to find anything against him." Bernardin could certainly have been forgiven if he had boiled over, harbored hatred for Steven Cook and for the greedy lawyer, Steven Rubino, and the rogue priest, Charles Fiore, who helped fan the flames. But no. No grudge. No resentment. No nursing the wounds. Nothing but prayer and kindness and honesty.

The sound bite that means so much, though, is this. "Joseph accepted the storm," Kennedy writes, "as part of what God asked him to experience as a condition of his service to the Church. He did not understand what Providence was preparing him for—that became clear . . . later—but he made the turmoil the fundament of his spiritual life instead of cursing the unfairness of its focus on him. He began each day now with an hour of prayer, and his calmness flowed from the sure sense he had of giving himself over to God's will, no matter what it was."

Now, what's this all about? About a year later, Joseph Bernardin was hit with pancreatic cancer. Fast-growing pancreatic cancer. No matter what they did—and the doctors did suggest some hopeful things—it would be this cancer which would end his life. Kennedy writes: "It seemed so unfair—as guileful as this disease that had entered him like an evil spirit—that Joseph, who had just come through the worst of tests, should have crashed through the paper-veiled hoop of a cruel circus only to find death, sharp of claw and uncaged, waiting for him."

And two years later, on November 14, 1996, Bernardin—*My Brother Joseph*—was gone.

But here's what this all means to us today. A situation comes along which is so unfair. It is! It's "in your face" unfair! And you deal every day, every hour, with the injustice of it all: how that other person gets away with hurting you, how they get the blessings you deserve, while you end up with the scorn that should be applied to them. So you're tempted to hold a grudge, to nurse your hurt feelings, to think of ways to get revenge. Of course you do. We all want to respond that way.

But what a picture we find in this quiet story, where a man of God looks at the TV cameras, and at the pictures of him splashed all over the front pages of every major newspaper—filled with lies—and says to himself: "What is Providence preparing me for? What does God want me to learn? Why is heaven allowing me to receive this spiritual discipline?"

I know of people who have enjoyed good, prosperous, well-ordered lives . . . except for this one certain person in their sphere. One person who hurts them. One person whose behavior always troubles their soul. One person who is unfair and insensitive. And for years they simply have to deal with it: either in the workplace, or in the church, or in the family. And instead of cursing and fretting and allowing that grudge to occupy an expensive bed in the Urgent Care center of their mind, they simply ask God in their prayers: "Father, what is it You want me to learn from this? I'm ready to sit at Your feet and be instructed through this experience. Open my mind up to discover and develop the character traits—patience, prayer, forgiveness, a heart to understand others, whatever—that You see I still need more help to fine-tune."

And sometimes it's simply a case of toughening up. Letting those boisterous waves roll against you while you try to stand against the currents of cruelty and accusation. Like Bernardin, you find yourself praying an hour a day now, instead of five minutes. You make this "turmoil the fundament of" your spiritual life.

Job got there, when he finally said about God: "Though He slay me, yet will I trust in Him."

Peter got there, after having the trials of his walking-on-water failure—speaking of boisterous waves—and his denial of Jesus finally prepare him for the real battles that faced him in the early Christian church. Later, in his first epistle, he wrote this: "In this [God's inheritance for us] you greatly rejoice, though now for a little while you may have had to suffer grief in all kinds of trials. These have come so that your faith—of greater worth than gold, which perishes even though refined by fire—may be proved genuine and may result in praise, glory and honor when Jesus Christ is revealed" (1:6, 7).

C. S. Lewis, in writing to that American woman whose middle name seemed to be Grudge, shares this encouragement: "It is very hard to believe that all one's indignation is simply bad: but I suppose one must stick to the text 'The wrath of man worketh not the righteousness of God.' I suppose one must keep on remembering that there is always something deeply wrong inside with a man so bad as this." Now notice this close: "For yourself I can only hope—and passages in your letter confirm my hope—that through all this you are being brought closer to God than you could have otherwise."

Wouldn't you like to be closer to God? To have, as Joseph Bernardin did, that quiet, "tensile strength"? Sometimes we only get strength to stand against the wind . . . when there *is* wind.

17

CHAPTER

Beanball
Mathematics

*The math of this world says, "Pay back everything." If someone
gave you a $20 hurt, you give them one right back. You don't dis-
count your revenge even a single nickel. A beanball for a beanball,
an eye for an eye. But we're about to graduate to an entirely new
system of math.*

Professional baseball is a universe where the concept of grudges
and getting even thrives in fine form. In George Will's spicy baseball book, *Men at Work,* he interviewed manager Tony LaRussa,
who was, at the time, the skipper of the Oakland A's. And LaRussa
confessed quite cheerfully that there was a precise science, a mathematics, to the idea of revenge. It's common knowledge that if the
pitcher on the opposing team hits one of your batters, knocks
him down with a pitch, you're going to get even. Are you going to
just forgive this guy, let him off the hook? Don't be stupid.

But what if your guy gets plunked, and it's in the eighth
inning of a crucial game where you're just ahead 2-1? All you
need to get is three more outs. Are you really going to risk the
game itself by hitting one of those three hitters, putting him on
base, just to "get revenge"?

"Who should make the decision whether you retaliate?" LaRussa asks. "It's got to be the manager. Sometimes you walk up to your player who got hit and say, 'I really believe this guy took a shot at you. We'll get somebody in the first inning to-morrow.'"

But there's a bit more to the marvelous mathematics of major-league baseball. "LaRussa is a stickler for proportion-ality in punishment," George Will writes. "'You try to match, as best you can. If they take a shot at your big producer, then you take a shot at their big producer. If they've just cold-cocked McGwire'"—who used to play for the A's back then—"'and their first batter in the inning is their light-hitting sec-ond baseman, that's not the guy. If someone takes a shot at Walter Weiss, then you look for their promising rookie or their second-year player who is a big star.'"

In other words, you've got to pay back by hitting the same caliber player who got hit on your side. Superstar for superstar, shortstop for shortstop, rookie for rookie. By that theory, if McGwire got hit in the seventh inning, and I was Sammy Sosa coming up to bat in the next inning, I'd just as soon phone it in. Because the math of baseball says I'm not going to get a hit— I'm going to *get* hit.

Well, it's kind of amusing to read, and you wonder who keeps the records: "Uh, Skip, we owe the Mariners one bop on the thigh and a beanball on somebody's shoulder in this game. That's left over from last season when we never paid them back." That kind of thing. But how often do we live this same way in our own lives away from the base paths? If somebody does you dirty to the tune of fifty bucks, don't you think about some way to get exactly that even? Fifty for fifty? Like the fictional George Constanza, who says to the pharmacy clerk on *Seinfeld:* "This isn't over. You have my ten dollars. You may think it's over, but it isn't. I will get that money back." And he devotes his every waking moment to scoring ten dollars' worth of revenge against that store, by shoplifting it or whatever. If your enemy insults you, you carefully weigh exactly how hurt you are, and you want to hurt him back that much . . . if not a bit more. Slugger for slugger, rookie for rookie. And as we've already found out, this mathematical framework simply does not work. It leaves everybody bruised and battered, both in body and soul. The math of revenge is a universal failure, and in our hearts we know it.

Let me take you back to where we started, though: the incredible Christian book, *Dead Man Walking*, written by Sister Helen Prejean. A man named Lloyd LeBlanc went through the horror of a missing son. No one knew where David was, what had happened to him. Was he just missing? Kidnapped? But then the dreaded phone call came from the police. "We think we've found your boy's body." Some nameless, faceless, evil monster Out There someplace had done this, killed his son. The love of his life, the light of his existence . . . gone.

Now according to the math of the Oakland A's, and the other twenty-nine baseball clubs, and the world, Lloyd LeBlanc would have just one choice: to hate and burn with anger until the wonderful day came when he could stick a knife into Patrick Sonnier and see his life ooze away. Until the day when he could take a shotgun and blow that miserable creep's head off. Until the day, April 5, 1984, when he could watch as prison officials at Angola hit the switch that electrocuted inmate #95281. That's the math of the world; that's what this grieving father had. Sonnier killed my boy; now I will participate mentally and morally and spiritually in wanting him dead. Life for life, pain for pain, tear for tear. I will get even; I will balance the scales.

But remember, Mr. Lloyd LeBlanc was a Christian man, not a pitcher for the Oakland A's. The mathematics of the gospel was supposed to be different for him. Read on, though, if you didn't see the film, and try to picture the scene in your own mind. "Lloyd LeBlanc says"—this is Sister Helen writing—"that when he arrived with sheriff's deputies there in the cane field to identify his son, he had knelt by his boy—'laying down there with his two little eyes sticking out like bullets'—and prayed the Our Father."

Can you visualize it? Dad kneeling in the dirt over the life-less corpse of his boy. And instead of thinking of revenge, of murder, he begins to pray the Our Father. He's a good Catholic man, and the words of the Our Father are what govern his life. At least they're supposed to. And so he begins: "Our Father, Who art in heaven, hallowed be Thy name."

It would be hard at that moment not to fall down in the dirt and instead scream at heaven: "My Father? Where were You, Father, when this happened? Why did You let my boy die? Damn You!" But Lloyd prays. "Hallowed be Thy name. Thy kingdom come, Thy will be done, on earth, as it is in heaven. Give us this day our daily bread . . ."

And I cannot imagine the universal pause that must have followed next. The angels must have bent low; Jesus must have drawn very near; God Himself must have come down from heaven to that cane field to listen to this incredibly brave man. Would he resort to anger, to the bitterness of hate, to the street mathematics of this battle-weary world? Or would Lloyd LeBlanc finish his prayer? And after a mo-ment, after that pregnant pause, that precious, horrible moment of weighing the cost, Mr. Lloyd LeBlanc went on: "And forgive us our trespasses . . . as we forgive those who trespass against us."

He said it. He actually said it. In fact, I didn't really tell it right, because Helen Prejean says that when Lloyd got to that line, *he did not halt or equivocate.* "Whoever did this, I forgive them," he said. On April 5, 1984, midnight in the Angola Penitentiary execution chamber, when Patrick Sonnier, moments away from death, said to him: "Mr. LeBlanc, I want to ask your forgiveness for what me and Eddie done," this Christian man nodded, "signaling a forgiveness he had already given."

And here at the close of our hard adventure together, friend, I guess I just want to say this. The Bible doesn't invite us to forgive because it will make us happier. To use forgiveness as a coping technique, a mental game, a psychological tactic of conflict resolution. I read what this Christian man did in that cane field, and I realize that we are being invited to actually move to an entirely different kingdom. It's as mind-blowing as that. "Father, forgive them" is the eternal foundation of a different kingdom . . . a kingdom not of this world. And we're invited to move to this amazing place.

A few years ago I took on the seven-week challenge of writing about some of Jesus' best parables. I discovered that these stories teach, over and over, the math of a faraway kingdom. A guy works one hour and gets paid for the whole day: that's heaven's math in heaven's kingdom. A prodigal son totally blows his dad's fortune, but gets forgiven. Gets a whole new fortune. Heaven's math in heaven's kingdom. People with no money, no tuxedos, no tickets, all invited to a black-tie wedding feast. Heaven's math. The first shall be last, and the last first. Heaven's math. Nails are being driven into your hands and feet: "Father, forgive them." Heaven's math in heaven's kingdom. Your worst hurts and hatreds given to a strong Father: "Dad, You take care of this." That's what you can say when you move to this wonderful, distant, different kingdom.

And you'd never want to go live there, and say, "Father, forgive them," unless you were sure Dad could take care of it.

If you enjoyed this book, you'll enjoy these as well:

Music Wars
David B. Smith. A balanced and grace-full discussion of contemporary versus traditional music. Smith addresses our inward attitudes about worship itself—its purpose and function. And what a sincere Christian should do who honestly does "hate that music!"
0-8163-1824-7. Paperback.
US$1.99, Cdn$2.99.

The Eleventh Commandment
Dwight Nelson. With memorable illustrations and a powerful new parable for today, Nelson shows us the secrets of abiding in Christ and reflecting His love to a suffering world in desperate need. A radical new look at loving your neighbor as yourself.
0-8163-1850-6. Paperback.
US$10.99, Cdn$16.49.

See With New Eyes
Ty Gibson uses striking language and illustrations to lead the disillusioned and the discouraged to a new vision of God that will change their hearts and their relationships with people around them.
0-8163-1786-0. Paperback.
US$11.99, Can$17.99.

Order from your ABC by calling **1-800-765-6955**, or get online and shop our virtual store at **<www.adventistbookcenter.com>**.

• Read a chapter from your favorite book
• Order online
• Sign up for email notices on new products